50p

Jacob
Williams
CCS

SEMINAR STUDIES IN HISTORY

The Origins of the
First World War

SEMINAR STUDIES IN HISTORY

General Editor: Roger Lockyer

The Origins of the First World War

Gordon Martel

LONGMAN
London and New York

LONGMAN GROUP UK LIMITED
Longman House,
Burnt Mill, Harlow, Essex CM20 2JE, UK
and Associated Companies throughout the World.

Published in the United States of America
by Longman Inc., New York

© Longman Group UK Limited 1987

First published 1987
ISBN 0 582 22382 2

Set in 10/11pt Baskerville Roman, Linotron 202

Produced by Longman Group (F.E.) Limited
Printed in Hong Kong

British Library Cataloguing in Publication Data

Martel, Gordon
  The origins of the First World War. –
  (Seminar studies in history)
  1. World War, 1914–1918 – Causes
  I. Title   II. Series
  940.3'11   D511
  ISBN 0-582-22382-2

Library of Congress Cataloging in Publication Data

Martel, Gordon.
  The origins of the First World War.
  (Seminar studies in history)
  Bibliography: p.
  Includes index.
  1. World War, 1914–1918 – Causes.   2. Europe – Politics
and government, 1871–1918.   I. Title.   II. Series.
D511.M269   1986   940.3' 11   86-3033
ISBN 0-582-22382-2

Contents

Seminar Studies in History
Founding Editor: Patrick Richardson

Introduction

The Seminar Studies series was conceived by Patrick Richardson, whose experience of teaching history persuaded him of the need for something more substantial than a textbook chapter but less formidable than the specialised full-length academic work. He was also convinced that such studies, although limited in length, should provide an up-to-date and authoritative introduction to the topic under discussion as well as a selection of relevant documents and a comprehensive bibliography.

Patrick Richardson died in 1979, but by that time the Seminar Studies series was firmly established, and it continues to fulfil the role he intended for it. This book, like others in the series, is therefore a living tribute to a gifted and original teacher.

Note on the System of References:
A bold number in round brackets (**5**) in the text refers the reader to the corresponding entry in the Bibliography section at the end of the book. A bold number in square brackets, preceded by 'doc.' [**doc. 6**] refers the reader to the corresponding item in the section of Documents, which follows the main text.

ROGER LOCKYER
General Editor

Part One: The Problem

1 The Outbreak of War

At 10 a.m. on 28 June 1914, Archduke Franz Ferdinand, heir to the Austrian throne, arrived in the town of Sarajevo in Bosnia for an official visit. While he and his party were proceeding along the main street of the city in open motor-cars, a young man stepped out of the crowd to throw a bomb at the Archduke. The bomb exploded, missed its target, and the would-be assassin was seized. The Archduke calmly ordered that the journey continue to the town hall where he endured a speech by the mayor, full of irritating references to the loyalty of the Bosnian people and their enthusiasm for his visit. Leaving the town hall, he insisted that he wished to visit the hospital to see one of his entourage who had been injured by the exploding bomb. As the party retraced its route along the main street, some confusion occurred, which resulted in the Archduke's car having to stop and reverse. At this moment another assassin stepped forward and shot Franz Ferdinand in the throat; within minutes both the Archduke and his wife lay dead; in less than five weeks Europe was at war.

The Austrians responded rather slowly to the assassination. Franz Ferdinand was, for a variety of reasons, not a popular man in court circles in Vienna, nor was there an overwhelming cry for revenge among the peoples of Austria-Hungary. In the government, however, there was a strong conviction that Serbia was somehow responsible: the assassin and his compatriots were Serbian nationalists, members of a terrorist group called the 'Black Hand', and the only question asked in Vienna was how far, and how fast, to move in crushing the threat to the monarchy posed by Serbian nationalism. Although they lacked proof of complicity on the part of the Serbian government, the Austrians agreed, on 19 July, to despatch an ultimatum that they could be certain Serbia would reject. The terms, had they been accepted, would have ended Serbia's existence as a sovereign state. The ultimatum was presented at 6 p.m. on 23 July; the Serbs were given forty-eight hours to comply.

Three hours before their reply was due, the Serbian government ordered the mobilisation of their army; but they also presented a note to the Austrian government couched in sufficiently ambiguous terms to convince some that they had accepted the Austrian demands. While the Austrians pondered the meaning of this reply they ordered the mobilisation of seven army corps against Serbia. The following day the Russian government decided to undertake various preliminary measures that would enable them to carry out a full mobilisation, should it prove necessary to support Serbia against an Austrian attack. At 11a.m. on 28 July Austria-Hungary declared war on Serbia. Later that day Russia announced her decision to mobilise, but only in those districts that would make possible a war with Austria-Hungary. This was duly undertaken at midnight on the following day. On 30 July the Russian government decided that a partial mobilisation would place them in a perilous position, should Germany come into the conflict; they therefore decided to order a full mobilisation.

The next day Austria-Hungary ordered a general mobilisation. With war between the Russians and the Austrians now apparently inevitable, the Germans ordered their army to mobilise and despatched an ultimatum to Russia demanding the immediate cessation of all military measures against Germany and Austria-Hungary within twelve hours. When the Russians failed to reply to this ultimatum, the Germans declared war at 6 p.m. on 1 August. The French ordered a general mobilisation on the same day; the Germans declared war on them two days later. On the morning of 4 August German troops crossed the Belgian frontier; by midnight Germany and Great Britain were at war.

Even such a superficial summary as the above indicates some of the complexities involved in answering the simple question, 'how did the war begin?' No one, not even the Austrians, went to war for the sake of Franz Ferdinand; and yet it was his violent death that initiated the diplomatic crisis that led straight to war (**278**). There was clearly more to the crisis than meets the eye – more than ultimatums and mobilisations. Why did the Austrians undertake to abolish Serbian sovereignty? Why did the Russians decide that they must support the Serbs against the Austrians? Why did the Germans believe that they must participate in what might have been limited to an Austro-Russian war? Why did the French mobilise their forces when war broke out in the east? Why did the British intervene in the conflict for the sake of Belgian territorial integrity? Or did they? In order to answer these questions we must unravel the diplomatic relations that connected these events to one another; we must understand what the 'alliance system' was and how it bound – or failed to bind – states to one another.

But statesmen seldom act on the basis of simple legal calculations. Even if we succeed in unravelling the complicated series of alliances and alignments that bound the states of Europe to one another we shall discover a new set of deeper, more fundamental questions that require answers if we are to understand how a great European war began in August 1914. How important was the phenomenon of nationalism? It was certainly the force that propelled the young Serbs into assassinating the Archduke – but why did the Austrians regard this force as dangerous to themselves? Did the Russians respond because of diplomatic commitments or because they regarded themselves as the patrons of Slavic brotherhood? How important was militarism? The states of the European continent had amassed standing peacetime armies of unprecedented size. Did this make war among them inevitable? Why did millions of young men readily assent to serving for one, two, even three years in the armed forces of their nation? Does this indicate a popular tide of warlike enthusiasm among the peoples of Europe that overwhelmed the statesmen of 1914? And what about imperialism? The late nineteenth century was the great age of European dominance: Africa had been partitioned, much of Asia was ruled by Europeans; the Ottoman and Chinese empires appeared to be on the verge of collapse. Was the war within Europe really a struggle for spoils beyond it? There were certainly a number of deeply-rooted forces operating in the summer of 1914, forces that altered perceptions, stimulated ambitions and generated fears, and any attempt to explain the origins of the war must take them into account.

Unfortunately for the student, the greater the gap in time between himself and his subject, the more difficult it is to recapture the emotions and the ideas that made up the frame of reference by which people judged the events happening around them. Two world wars, numerous revolutions, a great depression and the advent of atomic weapons separate us psychologically from the men and women of 1914. It is difficult to imagine now the kind of thinking that led people to rejoice at the prospect of war – but rejoice they did: there was dancing in the streets and spontaneous demonstrations of support for governments throughout Europe; men flocked to recruiting offices, fearful that the war might end before they had the opportunity to fight; there was a spirit of festival and a sense of community in all European cities as old class divisions and political rivalries were replaced by patriotic fervour. The student who seeks to understand 1914 must constantly remind himself of the emotional distance between him and his forebears.

This emotional distance can also be seen as an advantage. The question of how the war began was frequently posed in a different way in the aftermath of the war; the question asked was not so much how it began, but who was responsible. In Germany this was known as the *Kriegschuldfrage*, the 'war guilt question', which arose because the Allied states justified the demand for reparations embodied in the Treaty of Versailles by holding Germany responsible for the war. Thus, the question of war guilt was the most hotly debated historical controversy in the era between the wars. Those who regarded Versailles as an illegitimate, wicked peace, as a *diktat* imposed upon the vanquished, believed that if they could show that the burden of responsibility rested more with the Allied states than with the Central powers (or at least that responsibility must be shared equally), then the peace settlement might be revised and a morally defensible system of international relations put in its place. Conversely, those who believed that the power of Germany had to be permanently checked, and that the Austro-Hungarian monarchy was an evil and decadent empire that must give way to nation-states, sought to prove that the Central powers were responsible for the war (**7, 122**).

Thus, with some exceptions, the treatment of origins ran along predominantly national lines after 1919. Led by Germany, each state began to compile documentary collections of diplomatic correspondence in the hope that these would demonstrate their innocence. But no one was found innocent. The documents revealed an extremely complicated diplomatic system, a network of alliances and alignments and a variety of conflicting ambitions and fears. These complexities made it increasingly difficult to adhere to the view that any one state was responsible for the war. They also made it difficult to decide where the story of 'origins' ought to begin.

Few things reveal more about a historian's attitude to his subject than his decision on where to begin; and much of the debate over the origins of the war can be summarised by looking at the various starting-points that have been selected in the past.

Some historians have, in spite of the concern with 'underlying' causes, concentrated their attention on the summer of 1914. Historians who begin here seldom believe in the inevitability of the war. They resist the suggestion that it was intrinsic to the nature of the European states system. Instead, they argue that, had it not been for the peculiarities of the July crisis, war might have been avoided. This view places the burden of responsibility on one or more of the men who actually made the decisions that summer: on Count Berchtold of Austria-Hungary for his determination to crush Serbian independence; on Sazonov of Russia for his decision to support Serbia by attempting a partial mobilisation of Russian forces; on Kaiser Wilhelm of Germany for pushing Austria into taking a hard line in the crisis; on Raymond Poincaré of France for assuring Russia of French support for her policy in the Balkans; and on Sir Edward Grey for failing to either restrain Russia or warn Germany that Britain would fight alongside Russia and France should war break out in eastern Europe. Concentrating on 1914 does not, therefore, imply that any particular state or statesman was responsible for war, but it does strongly suggest that this crisis could have been managed successfully, as had others in the past.

Few historians today are satisfied with this concentration on the July crisis; almost everyone sees it as a logical culmination rather than a cause (**68, 81, 87**). Most historians think the story must begin earlier on, at least as far back as 1902–1907 and the 'diplomatic revolution' of those years. During this crucial period Great Britain, it is argued, departed from her policy of 'splendid isolation' to create an alliance with Japan and to arrange 'ententes' with France and Russia. This change in British attitudes can be interpreted either as a wicked imperialist plot designed to encircle Germany or as a necessary defensive response to the threat of German expansionism in Africa, the Middle East and Asia. German attitudes, it has also been argued, were undergoing a profound change at the same time: she was adopting a 'world policy', which reflected her determination to break out from her difficult position in central Europe, and which was symbolized by her decision to build a great navy. This concentration on the years 1902–1907, by focussing attention on the Anglo-Japanese alliance, the Anglo-French entente, the first Moroccan crisis and the Anglo-Russian entente, usually reveals a belief that the First World War was fundamentally an Anglo-German confrontation, a competition for empire outside Europe.

Other historians see the war not as the logical outcome of the Anglo-German naval race, but as the inescapable confrontation of two great alliance systems on the European continent. Consequently, they begin their story in the period 1879–1894. In 1879 the Dual Alliance of Austria and Germany was established, a defensive arrangement providing against an attack by Russia, or an attack by France supported by Russia. Three years later this was expanded into the Triple Alliance when Italy joined. As long as Bismarck was around to guide the alliance, and as long as he was able to remain on good terms with Russia, it seems – to most historians – to have posed little danger to peace. But with the coming to power of Wilhelm II a 'new course' was initiated in German foreign policy which led to the dismissal of Bismarck and the end of Russo-German harmony. Russia, by 1892, had aligned herself with France; by 1894 a formal Franco-Russian alliance had been established, and henceforth Europe was clearly divided into two armed camps. A spark, falling in the right place, could set off a European conflagration at any moment. The 'alliance system' has, in itself, often been regarded as a cause of the war, almost in isolation from the policy of any single state.

More direct responsibility is proposed by those who begin their account in 1870–71, which is regarded as a decisive turning-point because of the dramatic victory of Prussia over France. Those who see the First World War arising logically from the growth of German power are naturally inclined to interpret the creation of the German empire in 1871 as the proper starting-point for their account. The astonishing speed with which France, hitherto regarded as the greatest of European powers, was completely defeated by Prussia, indicated that the new German state might soon be in a position to dominate the continent. On the other hand France, humiliated by her defeat and deprived of Alsace-Lorraine by the Treaty of Frankfurt, followed a policy of revenge that would lead to war, some argue, as soon as she felt herself strong enough to win. Those who begin in 1870–71 are inclined to regard either Germany or France as the state primarily responsible for war in 1914; but they may also attribute the war to the more general breakdown in the balance of power that had kept Europe relatively peaceful since 1815 (**92, 93**).

The farther back in time historians go in tracing the story of origins, the more likely it is that they see general, underlying causes as the proper explanation of the war. Thus, some see 1848 as a focal point: the crushing of liberal revolutions in central and eastern Europe bolstered the power of despotic and militaristic regimes in Prussia, Russia and Austria-Hungary. Others go back to 1815 and the Congress of Vienna, where the conservative statesmen responsible for the settlement of the Napoleonic wars attempted to turn the tide of history and repress the legitimate demand of nationalities for independent states of their own. Most of the international problems in Europe over the following century were caused by nations 'struggling to be free'. Others wish to go further still – sometimes back to the dawn of time. Studies such as Spengler's *Decline of the West* and Toynbee's *A Study of History*, popular in the period between the wars, argue that the war was symptomatic of the decline, or the end, of western civilization itself.

Like all accounts of the First World War, this one must begin somewhere, and I have chosen to begin with an account of the Great Powers up to 1900. I have divided the powers as they were to be found in 1900: the Triple Alliance, the Franco-Russian Alliance and Great Britain. I shall attempt to sketch the broad outlines of the foreign policy pursued by each of the states throughout the nineteenth century, the changes that occurred in the second half of the century, and how these changes led to the creation of the alliance system and alterations in what was referred to as the Balance of Power. In attempting such a sketch I shall pay some attention to the question of how 'internal structures' influenced the direction of foreign policy in each of the great powers – a subject that has been a leading preoccupation of historians over the past generation. Having established the state of affairs that existed in 1900, I shall then proceed to follow the course of events, the diplomatic rearrangements, crises and wars that led up to the July crisis (**76, 86, 97**).

Part Two: The Great Powers to 1900

2 The Triple Alliance

The stability of an international system usually breaks down when the growing power of one state destroys the old network of relationships upon which the system was based. In this sense, a state that expands its power through a growth in population, trade, prosperity, industry or territory may be responsible for the breakdown of a system, even if it is not guilty of it. Nor does the breakdown of a system make a great war inevitable; it does, however, make war more likely as those states that derived certain benefits from the old system calculate that it is worth the risk of defeat on the battlefield to prevent the establishment of a new system. It is useful, therefore, when considering the origins of any great war, to determine which states were expanding the base of their power, and which states felt threatened by this. It is also worth considering whether or not the expansive state is conscious of the need to create a new pattern of relations.

In the half-century leading up to 1914, there is no doubt that Germany was the most dynamic state within the European system. Contemporaries had some difficulty in assessing the changing nature of growing states outside Europe: the United States and Japan were puzzling to them, and few believed that these two states were worth analysing in any detail, as their conditions seemed too far removed from those of Europe for useful lessons to be gained. Nor, in the case of the United States and Japan, was it believed that they would have much impact upon the European system. Germany was another matter. No state was more closely watched than Germany after 1870. Anyone interested in military power, in politics, in economic change, felt that they must take the German example into account – if only to criticise and counter it. Everyone believed that they could learn from the German example, and German thought, literature and music enjoyed an unprecedented popularity. In the years following Germany's wars of unification, there was an underlying assumption spreading throughout Europe that Germany was the state capable of upsetting the foundations upon which the international system was built.

The three wars that Prussia fought to create the new German empire, against Denmark in 1864, against Austria in 1866, and against France in 1870, demonstrated her military prowess. No one was really surprised when Prussia, in alliance with Austria, defeated Denmark. But the speed and ease with which Austria was defeated startled onlookers, who had expected a relatively balanced conflict; and the Prussian success in the war with France was astonishing. Even in the 1860s France had been regarded as the greatest continental power and as the state most likely to upset the equilibrium, so her quick and comprehensive defeat by Prussia decisively altered attitudes to European relations. Prussia's victories also made it clear that defeat in war would bring about fundamental changes within the defeated state: Austria's defeat led to the *Ausgleich* (compromise) of 1867, France's to the formation of the Third Republic in 1871 (**88**).

The new German empire could, therefore, be regarded as a revolutionary power, overturning the established international order and fomenting radical political changes. This was a role that Germany's chancellor, Otto von Bismarck, was determined not to play. He believed that the new empire was imperilled, having defeated two of her three great neighbours, and that if Germany did not proceed cautiously she would encourage the formation of a coalition of France, Austria-Hungary and Russia, which she could not hope to match. Germany, in no position to fight a war on three fronts, needed time to consolidate the new empire, and this meant upholding the status quo, guaranteeing her neighbours that she had no further ambitions to pursue that would endanger their security or their political systems (**146**).

The method by which Bismarck chose to safeguard the new empire from her neighbours was a system of alliances. Believing that it was impossible to make France friendly he had, in the Treaty of Frankfurt, tried to make it as difficult as possible for her to undertake an offensive campaign against Germany: a large indemnity would throw French finances into chaos and consequently deprive her of the funds necessary to fight a great war; the annexation of Alsace and Lorraine would deprive France of rich territory and the most promising ground from which to attack Germany (**92**). But, in order to forestall a war of revenge (*révanche*), France must also be deprived of allies. Bismarck at first had to satisfy himself with vague declarations of friendship expressed by the emperors of Germany, Austria-Hungary and Russia when they met in 1872–73. This 'League of the Three Emperors' (*Dreikais-*

erbund) was not an alliance, but it was important in signifying that the Habsburg and Romanov rulers of Austria-Hungary and Russia did not regard Germany as an international criminal. This satisfied Bismarck until he realised that the French had recovered from the war more quickly than he had anticipated; he then chose to deprive them of their most likely ally, Austria-Hungary, by offering her an alliance in 1879 that, in effect, guaranteed her against attack by Russia [**doc. 1**]. He then sought to prevent this latter possibility by drawing Russia into a new *Dreikaiserbund* in 1881. Finally, Italy was drawn into the fold when she joined Germany and Austria-Hungary in the Triple Alliance of 1882 [**doc. 2**].

Bismarck's alliance system was a complicated series of checks and balances, but it achieved two essential objects: it deprived France of possible allies and it established the German empire as a responsible and respectable state eager to uphold the new status quo. These limited aims and the desire for respectability reflected the conservative nature of the new empire, which was, in essence, a coalition of the Prussian monarchy and large landowners [**doc. 3**]. These conservative elements had, ultimately, been willing to fight the wars of unification only because Bismarck had persuaded them that they were acting defensively, and that the alternative to his policy was unification from below, led by social revolutionaries. The new state, although it did contain some representative institutions, retained the essential ingredients of the old monarchy, leaving great authority in the hands of the kaiser, especially when it came to the making of foreign and defence policy (**149**).

As eager as the conservatives were to contain social revolution and preserve the old order, the new empire developed in such a way as to make this difficult to achieve. Industry, which began to grow quickly, stimulated the development of both the middle- and working-classes, who were increasingly likely to support liberal or socialist ideas antithetical to the old order. These classes were making the new Germany less rural and more urban, whereas the political hierarchy was based upon the old agricultural system. The new territories of southern Germany were richer, more industrial, more densely populated and more democratic than Prussia. In spite of Bismarck's achievements, therefore, Germany's ruling classes felt that there was a latent internal crisis unfolding within the empire as the new classes created by the industrial revolution came to challenge the basis of the Prusso-German system established in 1871 (**155, 169, 172**).

Ironically, this fear of a latent crisis ran parallel to a growing sense of power – a confusing impression of reality that existed most conspicuously in the mind of Wilhelm II, who became kaiser in July 1888. Throughout his reign, which lasted until 1918, Wilhelm was torn between his worries about a social revolution and his belief that Germany had it within her reach to become a great world power. By the time he acceded to the throne, Germany was the most populous nation in Europe, after Russia; she produced more coal, iron and steel than any other nation on the continent. The kaiser believed that Germany's new power made it possible for her to break free from Bismarck's cautious preservation of the status quo, for which he had relied particularly on the conservative friendship with Russia, preserved by acting as the 'honest broker' in disputes between the Austrians and the Russians in the near east. The kaiser, who accepted Bismarck's resignation in 1890, launched Germany upon a new course (*Neue Kurs*) in foreign policy, symbolised by his visit to the sultan in Constantinople in 1889. Germany herself had interests to develop in the near east, and these interests would be developed by strengthening the alliance with Austria and ceasing to worry about repercussions from Russia (**160, 166**). Wilhelm assured the Austrian emperor that Germany would mobilise her forces simultaneously with Austria, no matter what the issue; he declined to renew the Reinsurance Treaty of 1887 with Russia in which the two states simply promised not to attack one another [**doc. 4**].

The new course in German policy was undoubtedly instrumental in prompting the Russians to consider seriously the French suggestions for an alliance; within a year the French fleet was visiting Kronstadt; within two years France and Russia had constructed a military agreement. Rather than destroying the principles upon which the new course was founded, however, this new development in European politics merely served to confirm them. The kaiser had accepted the arguments of his general staff that it was now possible for Germany to fight a war on two fronts and that, in preparing for this, Germany ought to have an indivisible alliance with Austria-Hungary and an understanding with Great Britain. In the summer of 1892 General Schlieffen, the new chief of the general staff, argued that, as a two-front war was now inevitable, Germany had to plan accordingly. As it would be difficult to defeat Russia quickly, he proposed to deal first with France, defeating her quickly and decisively while standing on the defensive in the east. The Schlieffen plan guaranteed that any crisis that led to war with Russia would also lead to war with France: Germany could not run the risk of a 'localised' conflict (**162**).

Schlieffen's strategy required a larger army and, in July 1893, he got one. But there the expansion of the army stopped. By 1900 the German army was no larger than the French, and 300,000 men smaller than the Russian. After the First World War most of the German military blamed the politicians for permitting this relative deterioration of the army to occur. In fact, although Schlieffen himself always advocated an increase in numbers, his colleagues did not and, ultimately, the freeze on the size of the army was due to the general staff itself and their fear of the coming social revolution. Further expansion of the army would have required the admission of 'bourgeois' elements into the officer corps, which would dilute the social exclusiveness of the corps – currently consisting of the landowning classes – and propagate the liberal, democratic ideals popular among the middle class. Furthermore, an expansion in the number of conscripts would mean drawing in more men from the urban proletariat – many of them infected with dangerous ideas of socialism. These fears would have counted for less had there not been a widespread expectation of an impending social conflict in which the army alone could safeguard the monarchical-landowner state; if the troops were socialists, or if they were commanded by liberals, the army might prove incapable of preventing the revolution (**142, 143, 157, 158**).

Germany's diplomacy reflected this curious combination of strength and weakness. Her policy was predicated upon the assumption that she was strong enough to fight a two-front war, but too weak internally to go on increasing her army to match those of France and Russia [**doc. 8**]. The kaiser and the men close to him repeatedly resisted opportunities to abandon the principles of the new course, preferring instead to bolster it through a closer connection with Austria-Hungary, Britain and Italy. They were increasingly dependent on the Austrians who, if they broke away from the alliance, would destroy the keystone of the new course. Britain and Italy were important in this respect: if Austria-Hungary were certain that Italy would not attack her in the south in the event of a war with Russia, and that Britain would neutralise Russia at the Straits and in the Black Sea, then she would be more inclined to stick by the alliance with Germany.

Because Italy was competing with France for empire in the Mediterranean, it did not seem difficult to keep her within the fold of the Triple Alliance. Britain proved more difficult (**152**).

Wilhelm II had favoured a closer understanding with Great Britain since the beginning of his reign. If Germany's future lay in the near east and eastern Europe, Russia was clearly marked as her main competitor. As Anglo-Russian antagonism had been the most consistent element in international relations since the Crimean war, Wilhelm assumed that the British would be happy to join an anti-Russian league. Even with the French alliance, the Russians would not be in a position to withstand the combined efforts of Germany, Austria-Hungary and Britain in the near east. This arrangement would be so advantageous to the British, who must recognise the inevitability of an Anglo-Russian war over Asia, that they should be prepared to make concessions to the Germans outside Europe. Such co-operation would symbolise the success of the new course (**164, 176**).

The British, however, refused throughout the 1890s to be drawn in to the alliance, and the Germans were increasingly persuaded that they would join only if the consequences of remaining aloof appeared to be too dangerous (**124**). Herein lies the diplomatic origin of the 'risk fleet': Germany should build a naval force strong enough to ensure that Britain would not dare run the risk of war with her. This would draw the British into the alliance and encourage good behaviour in Asia and Africa. And a fleet-building programme offered a political advantage inside Germany, by holding out to the business men of heavy industry the promise of reliable, long-term profits through the increasing demand for iron and steel. In this way the monarchical state might be able to rely upon the support of industrialists as well as landowners (**141, 148, 163, 165**).

By 1900, therefore, Germany had maintained, and even extended, the principles underlying the new course in foreign policy that had begun with the accession of Wilhelm II. She had reaffirmed her commitment to Austria-Hungary, developed war plans based on the assumption of a two-front war, and increased her interests in the near east and in colonial expansion. She was the most dynamic element in the international system, and most of her leaders were convinced that they were at a crossroads, one of which led to world power and empire, the other to the minor status of a relatively small state in the centre of Europe. The question facing Germany, as Bernhard von Bülow, one of her foreign ministers, put it, was whether or not she would become 'the hammer or the anvil' of world politics (**142, 144, 147**).

The alliance of Austria-Hungary and Germany in 1879 ought to be regarded as one of the most surprising events in modern diplomatic history. It is a mistake to assume that the sharing of German language and culture would inevitably draw the two states together into some close political connection; in fact, throughout the first half of the nineteenth century, nationality did much more to divide the two states than it did to unite them. The rulers of the Habsburg empire recognised that any promotion of the idea of nationality as the principle upon which states should be erected would doom their empire to extinction, and no one saw this more clearly than Count Metternich, the leading conservative statesman in Europe from 1815 to 1848.

The Habsburg empire owed its creation to traditional dynastic customs; it was an empire made by marriage and inheritance, wars and diplomacy; and it is best thought of as a loose agglomeration of Habsburg 'lands', an interconnected series of properties belonging to the ruling family, not as a 'nation-state'. Although this family and the ruling élite around them was German, the empire, by 1815, included Hungarians, Magyars, Poles, Czechs, Slovaks, Rumanians, Croatians, Serbs and Italians. The empire may have been a state ruled by Germans, but it did not regard itself as a German state.

For this reason, Metternich was especially anxious in the years following the Congress of Vienna to prevent the idea of a 'German nation' from spreading. When Napoleon had cobbled together a series of petty principalities, fiefdoms and bishoprics in southern Germany into what he called the 'Confederation of the Rhine', he had given impetus to the idea being broadcast by philosophers like Herder and Fichte that the German people ought to be brought together within a single state. These territories, still linked together after 1815 in the new German Confederation (in the hope that it would provide a more successful barrier against renewed French expansion), became the seed-bed of liberal nationalism. Groups of university students, *Bürschenschaften*, were particularly active, thus attracting the attention of Metternich who undertook to quash their movement. In other words, the Habsburgs were determined not only to avoid leading the unification of the German people, but to actively prevent it (**187**).

Habsburg policy following 1815, therefore, was guided by a

reasonably coherent and consistent set of conservative ideas. Metternich supported or proposed various interventions on the part of European governments to put down liberal and nationalist revolts in Spain, Italy and Greece, assuming that if the principle of representative, constitutional, nationalist regimes took root along the empire's frontiers, it would be only a matter of time before the contagion spread within the empire itself. Italian nationalism was particularly worrying in this respect. The settlement of 1815 had awarded Lombardy and Venetia, the two most prosperous territories of the Italian peninsula, to the Habsburgs. The political divisions existing within Italy gave the empire security on her southern frontier. If the Italians demanded, and achieved, unification, this would deprive the empire of rich territories and make her vulnerable to attack in the south. As late as 1860, the empire was surrounded, on three sides, by a succession of rather weak states, and nationalism, especially of the German and Italian varieties, was the main threat to this happy state of affairs.

The glaring exception to this strategically beneficial condition was in the east, where there loomed the enormous potential of the Russian empire. The main reason why Metternich accepted Tsar Alexander I's rather muddle-headed proposal of a 'Holy Alliance' of Christian princes was his desire that Russia should firmly adhere to the principle of monarchical solidarity. The Holy Alliance became, in effect, a loose association of the Habsburg, Romanov and Hohenzollern emperors to uphold the settlement of 1815 in the face of nationalist and liberal pressures. But the Greek revolt of 1828 opened a fissure between Austria and Russia when the tsar decided to support the demand of the Orthodox Greeks for independence from the Muslim Turks. Metternich preferred to treat the sultan as a respectable monarch and as a necessary component of the international system. Support for Greek independence might well unleash similar demands on the part of other subject peoples – Serbs, Bulgars, Rumanians – in the near east, some of whom were to be found in the Habsburg empire. Moreover, if the rather weak and remote rule of the Turks were removed from the Balkans, and if this were replaced with Russian-sponsored regimes, the Habsburg empire would be made much more difficult to defend. This underlying fear for the future of the Balkans proved to be one of the most persistent elements in the pattern of international relations throughout the nineteenth century (**188**).

The fissure in the Holy Alliance was closed, temporarily, as a result of the revolutions of 1848. The Habsburg empire was almost blown to pieces: violence erupted in almost every city; in Milan, Prague, and Budapest, nationalist forces seized control and demanded their independence or autonomy. The Italians and the Czechs were suppressed only when the army resorted to the most brutal measures. But the strength of the army was not sufficient to suppress the Magyars of Hungary, who were defeated only when the tsar dispatched a force of some 200,000 men to assist his fellow monarch. Russia remained quiet, practically immune from the upheavals of the year of revolution. The conclusion seemed to be that the Habsburg empire was going to find it very difficult to survive in the face of these disintegrative pressures, and that she would come to rely more and more on the Russians propping her up.

This explains why Austria's behaviour during the Crimean war came as such as shock to Russia. The Russians assumed, after 1848, that the Habsburg empire was both weak and friendly. She proved to be neither. Austria, rather than supporting Russia in her war with Britain and France, took advantage of the situation in which she found herself by insisting that Russia must withdraw her forces from the principalities of Wallachia and Moldavia; otherwise Austria would join Britain and France. The Crimean war provided the Austrians with the opportunity of barracading the Balkans from further Russian adventures: the principalities were given their independence and re-named Rumania; Russian troops were not to be permitted to advance through them to Constantinople. With the revolutionaries of 1848 either in prison or in exile and with the Balkans cut off from Russia, Austria appeared, by 1856, to be in a much safer position than she had ten years previously.

But the failure of the revolutions of 1848 convinced many nationalists in the Italian and German states that they would never be successfully united from below, that it would take war and the connivance of one or two great powers to create a unified state. In the Italian case, this meant that the kingdom of Piedmont-Sardinia had to fight the Austrians for control of Lombardy and Venetia, and that she had to have the active co-operation of France. It is a particularly complicated diplomatic story, but the conclusion was that Austria was defeated in battle, lost the two provinces, and ceased to be an 'Italian' power. There remained, however, a size-able Italian population within the empire that could prove a focal point of future Austro-Italian disputes.

Within three years the Habsburgs also ceased to be a 'German' power. The war with Prussia in 1866, which Bismarck adroitly manoeuvred the Austrians into starting, was really a struggle for the future of Germany; it was to decide whether the German states were to be united under the aegis of Prussia, or whether they would remain a loose association of independent entities, informally presided over by Austria. Defeat on the battlefield was quick, decisive and final, and after 1866 it was clear that Austria was no longer in a position to compete with Prussia as an equal. Bismarck's moderate peace terms reflected the real purpose of the war: the German Confederation was to be dissolved and Austria was to be excluded from German affairs. If Austria were to seek revenge, therefore, it would not be to recover 'national' territory or to relieve the burden of harsh financial and military terms; a war of revenge required that Austria must determine to regain predominance within Germany. The perfect opportunity for this came in 1870 when Prussia was fighting France – but Austria was prepared to do no more than stand by and hope that the French would win their battle for them. When this hope was dashed, so were any remaining Austrian dreams of a recovery in Germany (**98**).

The events of 1866–70 caused a profound re-evaluation of Austria's position in Europe; they also caused Austria to be transformed into 'Austria- Hungary', henceforth referred to as the 'Dual Monarchy'. Following the loss of Italy in 1860, the emperor had attempted to strengthen the empire by creating a representative assembly, the *Reichsrat*. The leading nationalities of the empire were not satisfied with the reform, however: the Magyars, Italians and Croatians boycotted it; the Czechs, Poles, Serbs and Slovenes opposed it; the new assembly proved unworkable and was held partly responsible for the military failure of 1866. The following year a new system was introduced, a compromise (*Ausgleich*) that made the empire an association of two independent states, Austria and Hungary, sharing a common ruler. The two states were to have a common foreign policy, defence and finances, and a unique – and cumbersome – process was created to accomplish this. Every ten years the two states were to agree on joint expenses for foreign policy and defence; the ministers of foreign affairs, defence and finance were to be jointly appointed to both states, and these ministers had to meet once a year with the 'Delegations' (executive committees) of both parliaments which communicated with one another only in writing. The system of 1867, which was untidy and invited dispute, was made manageable only because the cabinet was not responsible to parliament, but to the emperor, and because emergency decrees provided that a cabinet could govern for some time without the support of the legislature (**184**).

Austrian strategists believed that the threat of a renewed revolution in Hungary had forced them to fight, in 1859 and 1866, with a severe handicap. The hope of accommodating the Magyars of Hungary to the empire was the primary objective of the 1867 compromise. But the accommodation caused some fundamental changes in policy. The Magyars were not interested in Germany and they were unwilling to make any sacrifices for the recovery of the monarchy's position there. This made an improvement in relations with the new German empire much easier to achieve. On the other hand, the Magyars and the Germans alike were sensitive to the fact that almost one-half of the empire's population was Slavic, which led them to fear that the spread of Panslavism would lead to the dismemberment of the Dual Monarchy. Given these attitudes, it is not surprising that the earlier tendency of Austria to see Russia as an enemy was confirmed, while the defeat at the hands of Prussia was soon forgotten or overlooked.

The Dual Alliance of 1879 was the logical culmination of this new direction in the policy of Austria-Hungary [**doc. 1**]. An alliance with a strong Germany now seemed to offer the best protection against Russia. Austria-Hungary was also anxious for the enlargement of the alliance in 1882 to include Italy [**doc. 2**]. The Austrians had been compelled, when fighting the Prussians in 1866, to keep a large army in the south; although they had defeated the Italians in the battle of Custoza, their ability to defend themselves against the Prussians had been seriously hindered. As the same formula would apply in a war with Russia, the Austrians were eager to ensure that their southern frontier would not need to be defended, and, as long as Italian ambitions were turned in the direction of France, the Italian population of the Dual Monarchy was less likely to prove troublesome.

Austrian foreign policy, which had been such a tangle of conflicting interests in Germany, Italy and on the eastern frontier, now became unusually simple and straightforward: its aim was to protect the monarchy from disintegration resulting from the forces of Panslavism and Balkan nationalism. Austria-Hungary thus became the leading supporter of the status quo in the near east – a policy that culminated in two 'Mediterranean' agreements with Italy and Britain in May and December of 1887. The Austrians were as eager as the Germans and the Italians to draw Britain into the Triple Alliance; but by 1896, after repeated refusals on the part of Britain, the Austrians came to believe that they were running too many risks for the sake of Britain and they declined to renew the Mediterranean agreement. In its place they substituted an arrangement with Russia in May 1897 whereby the two powers agreed neither to disturb the status quo in the Balkans, nor to permit anyone else to do so; the Balkans were, for the next ten years, 'put on ice'. By 1900 Austria was firmly committed to the Triple Alliance – but as long as the Balkans remained quiet and Russia conservative, it was most unlikely that the connection with Germany would lead the Austrians to undertake an adventurous policy (**184, 186**).

No less surprising than Austria-Hungary joining Germany in the Dual Alliance of 1879 was Italy joining Austria-Hungary in the Triple Alliance of 1882. The Austrians had led the opposition to Italian unification throughout the nineteenth century: the Italian lands of Lombardy and Venetia were recaptured from the Austrians only by force of arms, and the Austrians had frequently intervened against the liberal and constitutional movements in the peninsula since 1815. A considerable change in outlook was necessary in order for the Italians to overlook the recent past.

Moreover, Italian unification had not been completed in the wars of 1859 or 1866; 'unredeemed Italy' (*Italia irridenta*) remained. The Austrians continued to hold on to the Tyrol, Trieste and Fiume – all areas heavily populated by Italians. In some eyes, therefore, Austria remained Italy's principal enemy (**105**). But others had grievances against France. In exchange for French assistance to Piedmont-Sardinia in the war of 1859 against Austria, the Italians had ceded Nice and Savoy – each with sizeable Italian populations – to France. Some nationalists believed that Italy would not be complete until these territories were recaptured. The French had also damaged themselves in Italian opinion by maintaining and defending the papal possessions in and around Rome; in 1867 they had actually fought off an attack led by Giuseppe Garibaldi, the great Italian patriot, and then sent him into exile. Only when the French needed all available manpower in their war with Prussia in 1870 did they withdraw their troops from Rome and permit the Italians to capture it. In northern Italy, therefore, there remained lingering grievances against both Austria-Hungary and France, although most nationalists felt that the grievances against France were rather minor by comparison.

More than Nice and Savoy, more than the Roman affair, dreams of greatness in the Mediterranean divided Italy from France. One of the focal points of the Italian Risorgimento was the past greatness of Rome, which seemed to show what the Italian people could achieve if they were united and freed from foreign controls. Even the most fervent nationalists refrained from suggesting that it was possible to re-establish the Roman empire in Europe, but they did believe that Italy had a special mission to spread civilisation – and the Mediterranean territories of north Africa, where the Ottoman empire was slowly disintegrating, offered an attractive site for the demonstration of Italy's renewed greatness (**209**). The strongest component of Italian imperialism was backward-looking: visions of a *mare nostrum* were always stronger than coldly rational calculations of financial and economic benefits (**203**).

Italy, following unification, was more concerned with questions of prestige and status than any other great power, another reason for her ambitions in the Mediterranean. Indeed, the fundamental question facing Italy after 1866 was whether or not she was in fact a great power. She had been united by war, but not by victories: defeats on the battlefield were compensated for by victories in diplomacy. Judged by any of the usual criteria Italy was certainly 'the least of the Great Powers' in 1900: she had the smallest army; she was the least populous; her iron and steel production was not only the lowest, but amounted to only one-fifth of Austria-Hungary's, one-tenth of Russia's (**200**). Italy was still an agricultural nation, yet she did not produce enough food to feed herself; her railway system was undeveloped and inadequate; her ports had not been modernised; she could not supply her own energy needs (**207**). It is difficult to believe that Italy could be regarded as a great power when Spain and Belgium were not; and yet the Italians were determined to achieve this status by behaving in the way that great powers were supposed to behave (**205**).

An empire in the Mediterranean would go far to establishing Italy's claim to great-power status, and it was this factor that drew Italy into the combination with Austria-Hungary and Germany (**96**). Membership of the Triple Alliance itself did much to support Italy's claim to this status, and the terms of the 1882 agreement were highly attractive to Italy. In return for promising to support Germany should she be attacked by France, Italy received a guarantee of German and Austrian support should France attack her. The only real concession made by Italy was her promise to remain neutral if one of the other two members of the alliance were engaged in a war with a single power: in other words, she would not take advantage of a war between Austria-Hungary and Russia to attack the Austrians in the hope of redeeming Tyrol, Trieste and Fiume. In this first phase of the alliance, Italy's role was clearly defensive [**doc. 2**].

Italy, in spite of her limitations, had great ambitions. The original version of the Triple Alliance, which did nothing to promise that any of these ambitions would be fulfilled, would have to be revised if Italy were to succeed with her Mediterranean expansion. Some hint of this was given in 1887 when the Triple Alliance was renewed and a new agreement was arranged between Italy and Austria-Hungary that promised 'reciprocal compensations' should the status quo of the Balkans be altered. This did something to satisfy Italian hopes of expanding along the shore of the Adriatic. More encouraging still was a new agreement with Germany that promised both military assistance to Italy, should she become embroiled in a war with France over Tunis or Morocco, and diplomatic assistance in securing for Italy improvements in her frontier security and maritime position: i.e., the irredentist claims against France in Nice, Savoy and Corsica, and the Mediterranean ambitions in Tunis. After 1887 it appears that Italy stood to make substantial gains in the event of hostilities with France or a disturbance of the Balkan status quo. Italy was not one of the powers working to uphold the current territorial and political arrangements in Europe (**214**).

Italy's ambitions were limited only by her lack of power and her vulnerable geographical position. In spite of the favourable diplomatic arrangements with Germany and Austria-Hungary, few Italians believed that they could afford to engage in a war which found Great Britain on the other side (**204**). Many of Italy's largest cities (Naples, Palermo, Genoa, Venice), were open to naval bombardment; much of her limited railway system hugged the coastline; she depended on maritime commerce to make up for her inability to feed herself and for the absence of coal supplies with which to fuel her industry. Italy had to be certain, therefore, that in a war with France she could count on British assistance or neutrality. This hope was realised in the Mediterranean agreement of February 1887 which, although vaguely referring to consultation and cooperation, did draw Italy and Britain closer together. Italy, even more than Austria-Hungary and Germany, wished for Britain's entry into the Triple Alliance.

The question facing Italy in 1900 then, was whether or not her continued membership in the Triple Alliance would enable her to fulfil some of her ambitious plans for expansion. As long as Britain remained even an informal friend of the alliance it seemed a useful instrument. But, were Britain to switch sides, it would be a dangerous policy for Italy to run the risk of a war with both Britain and France. The other members of the Triple Alliance were keenly aware that Italy always had the alternative of joining France and Russia and focussing her ambitions in the Tyrol and the Adriatic rather than in the western Mediterranean. Italy was apparently locked into the Triple Alliance; in reality she would be tempted to disengage if it appeared too dangerous or if a more attractive offer were made (**200, 201, 206**).

3 The Dual Alliance

The joining together of France and Russia in the Dual Alliance of 1894 was an astonishing event in European diplomacy, and one that fundamentally altered the system of relations. Few observers thought such an alliance possible. Philosophically, France and Russia represented opposite ends of the political spectrum: France stood for revolution and republicanism, Russia for stability and despotism. Nor was this clash of ideas purely symbolic. Russian statesmen believed that all threats to the tsarist regime and to the stability of European politics emanated from Paris; French statesmen believed that their republican system and a morally legitimate European order would always be imperilled by the existence of the Russian autocracy. Nor were these fears merely symbolic: France had invaded Russia twice in the last century, in 1812 and in 1854; Russia had led the anti-revolutionary movement, creating the Holy Alliance in 1815 and crushing the Hungarian revolution in 1848. When the two states committed themselves to assist one another if attacked, therefore, they implicitly announced the triumph of interests over ideas. In order to understand the origins of the First World War it is essential to understand what these interests were and how each of these two Great Powers believed their alliance would provide for their achievement.

Foreign observers of nineteenth-century Russia were invariably struck by two features of Russia as a great power. Those from western Europe, especially from Britain and France, were struck by the nature of the tsarist autocracy, which seemed to them to give a distinctive colouration to Russian foreign policy, designed as it was to protect the legitimacy of the regime. They were also sensitive to the enormous power of Russia, although observers from central Europe, especially from Prussia and Austria, were more likely to be fascinated by this feature. Whether this power was real or imagined, and whether or not the autocracy predetermined the course of Russian policy were crucial questions for European diplomats in the late nineteenth century.

The part played by Russia in the destruction of the Napoleonic empire contributed decisively to her reputation as a great power. Although Napoleon had defeated each of the states of continental Europe and proven himself invulnerable to the continuing enmity of the British, his *grande armée* had been annihilated in the attempt to invade Russia with the loss of 500,000 out of the original force of 600,000 men. Europeans as a whole drew two conclusions from this episode: the territorial expanse of Russia was so immense that a successful invasion was almost unimaginable; and the population of Russia was so great that she could suffer the most appalling losses and live to fight another day. Thus, although Napoleon penetrated as far as Moscow and captured the city, and although Russia lost 200,000 men in a single battle at Borodino, Russia was not defeated, and within three years 30,000 of her troops participated in the allied occupation of France.

Russia's advantages in men and territory persisted, or grew, throughout the century. Her territory dwarfed that of continental Europe. Her population, in 1900, was twice that of her nearest rival, Germany, and almost equal to the combined peoples of the Triple Alliance. In 1900 the Russian empire comprised some 16 million square miles and contained approximately 125 million people.

The raw components of power seemed to suggest that Russia was capable of overwhelming any potential opponents on the European continent, and the Germans and Austrians were certainly sensitive to the dangerous proximity of the Russian giant. But power, in order to be effectively applied, depends on more than size alone, and here contemporaries in 1900 were much less certain about the actual strength of Russia. Modern armies and navies were in the process of becoming industrial machines. They required railways and coal to move them, iron and steel to arm and supply them, and in these components of power, Russia was noticeably behind the other great powers. In 1910 European Russia had less than one-tenth the length of railway per square kilometre of Britain or Germany. In 1900 her coal production was one-half that of Austria-Hungary, one-tenth that of Germany; her pig-iron production amounted to 40 per cent of the German, 33 per cent of the British; steel production to 30 per cent of the British, 20 per cent of the German. Given Russia's limited industrial development, it was questionable whether she would be able to utilise her advantage in manpower, and it was clear that the most difficult operation for her to mount would be one that required her to go quickly on to the offensive (**215**).

Critics of the regime blamed Russia's weakness on her autocratic system of government. In the decade prior to the revolution of 1905 a wide range of opposition groups emerged, all of them demanding fundamental changes in the nature of the regime. Marxists established the Russian Social Democratic Labour Party in 1898, which aimed to overthrow the tsar by harnessing the revolutionary potential of the proletariat. Liberals published a newspaper, *Liberation*, beginning in 1902, and organised the Union of Liberation in 1904, which aimed to abolish the autocracy and establish constitutional government. Populists united several factions in 1901 when they organised the Party of Socialist Revolutionaries, dedicated to the triumph of the 'people's will' which was to be achieved through the use of terror and by mobilising the peasant masses of the countryside (**216**).

As varied as these opposition groups were, and in spite of their differences with one another, they were nevertheless united in their belief that social justice was impossible under the tsarist autocracy. Moreover, they believed that Russia could never be transformed into a modern state as long as the tsar and his gentry supporters remained in control. Thus, the Russian people would continue to find themselves at the mercy of their better-organised and better-equipped neighbours, as they had during the invasions of 1812 and 1854.

The tsar, by contrast, rested much of his right to govern upon the claim that he and his ancestors were responsible for the creation of the Russian state, and that the autocracy, in alliance with the gentry, was essential to the maintenance and defence of the state. This claim made the tsar and his advisers peculiarly sensitive to international questions. If the regime suffered a defeat in diplomacy the reverberations might shake the autocracy to its foundations: disenchantment within Russia was most intense in the immediate aftermath of disastrous foreign adventures – following the Crimean war of 1855–56, the war with Turkey of 1877–78, and the war with Japan in 1905. The tsar was fully alive to the dangers of adventurism, especially after 1905, but he was also aware that his other claim to authority, his leadership of the Christians of the Orthodox church, would suffer if he failed to act on behalf of his brethren when they were endangered by the Muslims of the Ottoman empire. Too cautious a policy might be as dangerous as one that was too adventurous (**217**).

These twin claims to authority, the traditional powers of the monarch and the leadership of the orthodox church, were nicely fused together in the Holy Alliance created by Tsar Alexander I in 1815. The Alliance, which initially included Russia, Austria and Prussia, was supposed to guarantee that Christian principles would provide the foundation for rule in these states, and that the monarchs would work together to maintain peace and justice. Monarchical solidarity was to take the place of revolutionary republicanism and nationalism, while the right to rule was to be based on Christianity rather than the Rights of Man or the General Will. In the years following the Congress of Vienna, Russia came to be regarded as the bastion of reaction, and the upheavals that did occur – in Spain, Italy, Germany – were far removed from her own frontiers. Never was the strength of tsarist rule so vividly demonstrated as in 1848, when, practically free from the revolutionary uprisings that swept across Europe, Tsar Nicholas I was able to dispatch 130,000 troops to assist the Habsburg emperor in crushing the Hungarian revolt (**220**).

The idea of the Holy Alliance was an attractive one to Russia, both because it upheld the principle of the Christian monarchy and because it offered protection against attack by her neighbours. It also appeared to provide a barrier against revolutionary infection from western Europe or against another Napoleon. It should not be surprising to discover, therefore, that some Russians in the decades before 1914 longed for a return to the peace and security of the Holy Alliance, to a policy of co-operation with Germany and Austria.

In spite of the alliance, there had always been an underlying tension between Russia and Austria arising from the growing aspirations of Balkan Christians to set themselves free from Turkish rule [**doc. 10**]. Where Austria preferred to quell upheavals and revolutions of any kind, Russia preferred to support the demands of the Christians, a policy which led to a particularly acute difference of opinion over the question of Greek independence in 1827. The tsar's inherited role of protector of the Christians in the Ottoman empire also led to war with Britain and France in 1854, when Nicholas I was led to believe that Napoleon III was attempting to replace him as spokesman for the Christians at Constantinople and that the sultan might thereby become a puppet of France and Britain. Equally important, the Crimean War killed the Holy Alliance. Austria refused to act as the friend of Russia – in spite of having been saved from dissolution six years earlier – and took advantage of her position to create a situation during the war and at the peace conference that was damaging to

Russian interests in the Balkans and in the Black Sea.

After the Treaty of Paris in 1856 Russian foreign policy became more 'realistic', less concerned with principles such as monarchical solidarity and orthodox rights, more concerned with the interests and the security of the Russian state. The Crimean War had shown that Russia was vulnerable to attack in the south through the Straits, and the treaty of 1856 had attempted to perpetuate this vulnerability by 'neutralising' the Black Sea: not permitting Russian or Turkish warships to operate there. If Austria was now seen as unreliable or unfriendly, Britain was now regarded as Russia's real antagonist, having achieved paramount influence at Constantinople and having apparently determined to use this influence to attack Russia in the Black Sea whenever she found it useful to do so. The new realism in Russian policy meant establishing a counterpoise to Britain in the Black Sea by undertaking a forward policy in central Asia in order to threaten the British empire in India (**98**).

The new realism also meant working closely with Bismarck. Prussia had not joined the Crimean coalition and, especially after the Austro-Prussian war of 1866, she seemed to offer a useful counterpoise to Austria. A strong tradition of germanophilia existed at the Russian court, Prussia had no ambitions in the Balkans or at the Straits, and the two states co-operated in subjugating their Polish subjects. Russia's realism was rewarded in 1870 when, in return for remaining neutral during the Franco-Prussian war, Bismarck led the way in securing international agreement to the annulment of the Black Sea clauses. As long as Bismarck was prepared to keep a close rein on Austria in the Balkans and to act as the 'honest broker' in differences between the two states, Russia continued to co-operate with him, and was even drawn into his Three Emperors' League in 1871.

But the *Dreikaiserbund* was not a renewed Holy Alliance. Russia never again trusted Austria after the betrayal of 1854–56, and the later nineteenth century witnessed the rise of the 'slavic idea' which saw Russia as a slavic state culturally distinct from the states of western and central Europe. Russia, according to this idea, had an historic mission to protect and promote – perhaps even to unite – all Slav peoples, which meant defending the interests of Bulgars, Serbs and Montenegrins. This idea, which was a more extreme version of the older notion of an Orthodox brotherhood, became increasingly popular among Russian educated classes, even though it inevitably meant antagonism with both the Ottoman and Habsburg empires. When Wilhelm II acceded to the Prussian throne in 1888 and quickly launched Germany on a 'new course' in foreign policy, a large part of which involved the expansion of German interests in the Ottoman empire and more straightforward support of Austria-Hungary, the germanophiles in Russia found it increasingly difficult to maintain the connection with Germany in the face of slavophile sentiments (**209**).

The *Neue Kurs* in German policy also reflected the changing nature of the balance of power in Europe. Germany's decisive victory over France in 1870–71 showed that Germany was now the pre-eminent military state on the continent and, over the next twenty years, the gap between the two continued to grow. Russian diplomats were increasingly convinced that Germany intended to harness this new strength: if Germany crushed France altogether she would be free to pursue an aggressive policy in the east. This was particularly true given the signs that the Habsburg empire was being transformed into a German satellite, rather than an equal partner, and that Britain was co-operating with the Triple Alliance in the near east and in the Mediterranean. A strong and independent France, even if she did follow the dangerous creed of republicanism, was seen by Russian diplomats as a necessary counterbalance to German power. Overcoming a century of tradition, therefore, Russia signed, on 4 January 1894, an alliance with France that provided for mutual defence against a German attack, or an Austrian attack supported by Germany, or an Italian attack supported by Germany [**doc. 6**] (**215**).

The French found it as difficult to overcome their aversion to the tsarist autocracy as the Russians had found it to overcome their horror of revolutionary republicanism. Throughout the nineteenth century, no state had so clearly symbolised the decadence of the old regime as Russia. She had a monarch who claimed that his right to rule came from God, whereas both Napoleon I and Napoleon III claimed their mandate came from the people. Russia was still stuck in the mire of unenlightened, theocratic ideas: the Orthodox church was the most backward in Europe; no representative institutions existed whereby the people could make their general will known; ordinary people were treated as chattels, not as citizens. The French came to believe that an implicit connection existed between the survival of the autocracy in Russia and the unregenerate nature of the whole European system. Paris, therefore, became the home of Russian revolutionaries: anarchists, nihilists and communists organised secret societies, published newspapers, and plotted the overthrow of the tsar with the tacit support of the French government. The cause of Polish nationalism was close to many French hearts, and France became the champion of the cause and the home of the movement. When Paris erupted in the final days of the Franco-Prussian war, forming a revolutionary commune, and when this was followed by the establishment of the third French Republic, it seemed to confirm the impression that France would always be inflammable, chaotic and fanatical.

Bismarck certainly hoped that this would be the case. Extremism would simultaneously, he believed, divide France internally and deprive her of allies. France must be kept weak because, after 1871, she would be determined to seek revenge for her defeat.

Although neither of Bismarck's hopes were fulfilled, the impression of French weakness has become indelibly etched upon the history of Europe from 1871 to 1914. In retrospect, however, this impression has less to do with political extremism than with the underlying factors that govern great-power status. At the time of the Franco-Prussian war, the two states had been roughly equal in population; by 1914 Germany was almost double the size of France, which was now only slightly larger than Italy, and smaller than Austria-Hungary. In both iron and steel production France and Germany were equals in 1870–71; by 1914 France produced only 30 per cent as much iron, 25 per cent as much steel. The balance that had existed at the time of the Franco-Prussian war had clearly disappeared by 1914, and the conclusion of contemporaries that France was no longer in a position to dominate Europe, and that in this she had been replaced by Germany, was certainly well-founded (**98**).

The weakness of France can be exaggerated, however, and it is important to recognise that few Frenchmen believed they were finished as a great power. The French in general, and republicans in particular, attributed their defeat in 1870–71 to the corruption and incompetence of Napoleon III and his advisers. France and Prussia were, it was held, equals in 1870–71, so defeat on the battlefield was not predetermined: rather, it had come about because of bad management and because the leaders of the nation were more concerned with their personal luxury and prestige than with the good of the nation. The leaders of the new republic aimed to create a regime that would be moral, efficient and unified, a regime in which all Frenchmen could take pride and which, consequently, would benefit from a renewed patriotic fervour.

The first problem confronting the new republic was the payment of the huge indemnity provided for in the Treaty of Frankfurt; until this was paid a German army of occupation would remain in France. Bismarck had hoped that the indemnity would throw French finances into such disorder as to make their recovery long and hard. The French people, however, unlike the Germans after 1919, chose to regard payment as a matter of national honour and, against all expectations, paid the indemnity in a little over two years – six months ahead of schedule. Nor did this impoverish the nation. Over the next forty years the French showed that, in spite of their lagging industrial productivity, they enjoyed sufficient reserves of capital (as a result of the national preoccupation with saving rather than spending) to remain a leading participant in the European economy. Iron and steel do not account for everything, and the ability of the Paris *bourse* to float loans was an important ingredient in the *rapprochement* that led up to the Franco-Russian alliance (**241**).

French money also made it possible to expand and modernise the army with unexpected speed, and to an extent that frightened Bismarck. Within a year of the French defeat, the new republican Chamber of Deputies agreed that they could afford to introduce compulsory five-year military service for all men between the ages of twenty and forty. For the next thirty years France consistently spent more on her army than Germany did, and at least twice as much on her navy. In 1900 she had slightly more men in her regular army than Germany. The tremendous growth of Germany's economy undoubtedly provided her with a greater potential, but this might count for little if she could be defeated quickly on the battlefield. The French devotion to defence was achieved at tremendous cost, as the individual Frenchman regularly paid almost twice as much as the individual German, and this undoubtedly contributed to the growing gap in the economic development of the two nations. Nevertheless, French patriotic pride combined with gold reserves to give France a military standing almost equal to that of Germany in 1900 (**224, 237**).

The revival of patriotism after 1871 also gave a new stimulus to colonial expansion. At the time of France's defeat, her overseas empire consisted of no more than a handful of ports and islands along the coasts of Africa and China; by 1900 the French empire had expanded to comprise four million square miles – an empire second only to that of Great Britain and more than twenty times the size of France itself. Vast territories were marked out in north Africa, west Africa and Indo-China, and a large navy was built to defend the new possessions. Until the late 1880s France was spending almost as much as Britain on her navy, and more than Germany, Austria-Hungary, Italy, Russia and the United States combined. This activity overseas, along with the reform and expansion of the army, the readiness to use accumulated capital for political purposes, and pride in the new republic, contributes to the picture of France from 1870 to 1900 as a spirited and determined state, eager to overcome the reputation for weakness and corruption that she had acquired as a result of the débacle of 1870 (**229, 236, 246**).

The great revival following 1870 was not, however, simple or straightforward. Colonialism brought quarrels with Britain, and almost led to war in 1898, whereas *révanche* persisted in seeing Germany as the real enemy, which led the Germans to anticipate that any conflict in Europe would encourage the French to attack them. Those who looked overseas for the future of France as a great power usually saw Britain as the enemy, and therefore supported the building of a large fleet; logically, it also ought to have led them to support a *rapprochement* with Germany in Europe. Those who believed that French power and dignity could be restored only by recapturing the lost provinces of Alsace and Lorraine clearly regarded Germany as the enemy, and therefore supported the creation of a large army; logically, it also ought to have led them to support the settlement of colonial differences with Britain overseas (**233, 238**).

From 1870 to 1900, however, the French attempted to pursue both a continental and a colonial policy. There was no clear or consistent leadership to provide a systematic approach to foreign affairs. Although the new regime proved to be stable, successfully withstanding challenges from monarchists and Bonapartists, the governments of the republic were much less so; they lasted for little more than a year at a time in the first two decades after 1871. France had thirteen different foreign ministers between 1871 and 1890. This political instability resulted in a confused policy that managed to antagonise both Germany and Britain, and contributed significantly to the Anglo-German harmony that prevailed throughout most of this period.

The decisive break with Britain came over the occupation of Egypt in 1882. When the Egyptian government was bankrupted in 1876, France and Britain had agreed on a joint financial control, but this broke down in 1882 when a nationalist revolt stirred the British to intervene by force. However, the French, who had promised to join in, were prevented from doing so by a vote in the chamber. Although the deputies were not prepared to undertake the expense of a joint occupation, there was widespread resentment at the establishment of British predominance in Egypt. Ever since Napoleon's invasion of 1798 the French had come to regard themselves as performing a special mission in Egypt. One of the glories of Napoleon III's Second Empire had been the building of the Suez Canal, and French investment in Egypt had continued to grow since 1871. Even if the deputies were not keen on occupation, the permanent officials of the Quai d'Orsay (the French foreign ministry), who really managed policy in the absence of strong governments, were mostly keen colonialists. Many officials believed that the way to restore French greatness was to establish a great empire in north Africa stretching from Morocco to Egypt, thus turning France into the greatest power in the Mediterranean. For twenty years following the British intervention, therefore, the foreign ministry was preoccupied with prying the British loose from Egypt (**230**).

The Germans, not surprisingly, welcomed the Anglo-French antagonism over Egypt, and Bismarck encouraged the French to enlarge their interests in Tunisia, Morocco, Nigeria, Madagascar and Indo-China. The years immediately after 1882 were ones of Franco-German *détente*. But French policy was inconsistent: *révanche* was not dead. Although a growing number of responsible French politicians were inclined to forget the lost provinces, few dared to proclaim this publicly; the cause of Alsace and Lorraine still fired the imaginations of too many Frenchmen for this to be a practicable programme, a point which was illustrated in the Boulanger affair of 1886–89. General Boulanger was an outspoken nationalist who, as minister of war in 1886–87, initiated further reforms and expansion of the army. He became an immensely popular figure, especially with those extreme patriots who were calling for an immediate *révanche*. Bismarck was particularly worried by his popularity, because it seemed to presage a Bonapartist revival: a strong man on horseback leading the country in an anti-German direction. Although Boulanger lost his nerve and abandoned the idea of a coup d'état, his momentary fame led to a new military law in Germany, which expanded the army, and to talk of a preventive war against France (**231, 240**).

The Boulanger affair made it clear to the Germans that any

détente with France would be short-lived; in spite of their colonial aspirations, the French, it seemed, would never be persuaded to think of Germany as anything but an enemy. By the 1890s few Frenchmen were prepared to undertake an aggressive campaign to restore the lost provinces – but few were prepared to abandon them permanently to Germany. The war-scare that arose from the Boulanger affair led the French to fear that the Germans would attempt to confirm their possession of Alsace-Lorraine by launching a new war against them (**232**).

In spite of the revival of French spirits, finances and military forces following 1871, France remained as isolated diplomatically as she had been during the war itself. Where Bismarck had succeeded in building the Triple Alliance and bringing Russia and Britain into association with it via the *Dreikaiserbund* and the Mediterranean agreements, the French had only managed to antagonise Britain and Italy. Fortunately, an alliance with Russia would not compel the French to choose between the colonies and the continent: the Russians had been consistently anti-English since 1856, and, with the abandonment of the Russo-German Reinsurance Treaty in 1891, the Russians were prepared to consider French suggestions for a defensive alliance against Germany. The alliance really did nothing to provide for *révanche*, but it did offer security against another German attack. Security in Europe encouraged the French to become more aggressive overseas, and within a few years they found themselves on the brink of war with Britain.

The French colonialists believed, after almost twenty years of fruitless diplomatic efforts to persuade the British to leave Egypt, that they must find some way to prod the British into serious negotiations. The strategy they resolved upon was to send a military expedition through the Congo into the Sudan. Here they could, by occupying a position at the headwaters of the Nile, threaten the British position in Egypt. They believed that only a threat would be necessary – but they were mistaken. When the French force arrived at Fashoda in September 1898 it was challenged by a superior British force, and the British government made abundantly clear its determination to go to war rather than permit the French to remain in the Sudan. The French, not prepared for war against Britain, had no choice but to back down and retreat from the Sudan (**248**).

By 1900, therefore, French policy was still uncertain. The colonial party used the example of Fashoda to encourage a *rapproche-*

ment with Germany and to argue that the alliance with Russia ought to be expanded to include the contingency of war with Britain. The Franco-Russian alliance was accordingly altered in this way in 1899. The object of the alliance was also expanded to provide for the maintenance of 'the balance of power in Europe' in the hope of forestalling direct German control of the Habsburg monarchy. Whether the French ought to concentrate on the German threat in Europe or the British competition in Africa had not yet been resolved. Temporarily, the French hoped that their alliance with Russia would prove strong enough to permit them to pursue both objects simultaneously.

4 Great Britain

Britain in 1900 was the only European great power not committed to one of the two rival alliances. She was instead committed to fighting a sizeable war in South Africa, a fact that led some critics of the government to deplore the 'isolation' that left her not only without allies, but practically without friends. Critics worried that this isolation would render Britain vulnerable, that the animosity felt for the British cause in the Anglo-Boer war might lead to the formation of a continental league aimed at the British empire – perhaps to a new version of Napoleon's continental system. After all, they pointed out, France and Russia, Germany and Italy, all coveted one or more of the territories contained within the empire. Nor was isolation necessary: Germany, Austria-Hungary and Italy had been attempting to persuade Britain to join the Triple Alliance for a decade or more. Britain, however, had steadfastly refused to join, and leading members of the government were, by the time of the Anglo-Boer war, proclaiming that isolation was 'splendid' (**256**).

Was it a sign of British strength or weakness that she was isolated in 1900? Continental observers of Britain in the late nineteenth century were particularly struck by three aspects of Great Britain as a great power: her industry, her empire and her navy. These components were understood to work in close conjunction with one another: her industry gave her the desire for empire, for the resources and markets it provided; industrial prosperity and technical efficiency made possible the construction of a large, modern navy; and the mastery of the seas provided by the navy enabled her to defend the empire against all opponents. This simplistic picture is misleading, but the idea that British power was fundamentally industrial, and that British interests were essentially imperial, was entertained by most observers of Victorian Britain. What was debateable at the turn of the century was whether or not British power was sufficient to enable her to stand aloof from the system of European alliances and alignments.

British industry was still pre-eminent in the Europe of 1900. She produced more coal than the five powers of the continent combined. She produced as much iron as the Triple Alliance, and only Germany produced more steel. In spite of the advantage she still enjoyed, however, the continental states in general, and Germany in particular, were rapidly closing the gap. In 1870 Britain was producing five times as much coal as all of Europe, and twice as much iron; in 1880 she was producing twice as much steel. British production in all of these vital sectors of the economy rose steadily in the fifty years prior to 1914, but by the time war broke out Germany was producing almost as much coal, more iron and twice as much steel. Moreover, in the newer, more technically-oriented chemical and electrical industries Britain was outdistanced from the start.

This changing pattern of production has led some commentators to argue that the First World War was simply an Anglo-German contest for industrial predominance and the trade that followed from it. But Russia too was making rapid strides in catching up with Britain and, outside Europe, the United States had already far surpassed Britain in all of the vital industrial components by 1900. In spite of the continuing prosperity of British industry in 1900, therefore, it is difficult to argue that it provided her with a clear advantage over potential rivals.

The British empire, on the other hand, appeared in a quite different light. Without the empire Great Britain was a state not much bigger in territory or population than Italy; with the empire she was bigger than Russia. The enormous extent of the empire, over ten million square miles, gave Britain potential reserves of manpower and resources not available to the continental states, and most particularly not to the central powers. Colonial groups in Germany, France and Italy argued that they too must acquire empire in order to compete with Britain. But the empire could also be interpreted as a source of weakness: Russia, the United States and France could endanger significant portions of the empire, and Britain, having fought each of them in the course of the nineteenth century, had to take defensive measures against these threats. Germany, Japan and Italy were now in a position to cause trouble and expense to the British, should they choose to do so. Britain had to erect fortifications and maintain defences in the far east, in central Asia, in Egypt, in the Mediterranean, in South Africa, and on the Pacific coast of North America – to name only the most prominent ones. Critics of empire within Britain, of whom J. A. Hobson was the most famous, argued that the expense of such undertakings was out of all proportion to the benefits gained, that empire was a source of weakness, not strength.

The greatest expense arose from the necessity of building a large navy to defend imperial possessions, and Hobson argued that naval interests – the Admiralty, shipbuilders and port towns – were among the select groups that actually benefited from empire. Radicals also argued that a large navy was not really essential for the defence of the British Isles; a small navy and defensive fortifications were sufficient to deter an invasion. But as the empire meant preparing for an imperial war, it was not enough that the British navy was superior to any European one; hers must be stronger than any possible combination of European navies. In the 1890s this meant building to the 'Two-Power Standard', to meet the possibility of a combined Franco-Russian threat. After the German naval laws of 1898 and 1904, Germany too had to be taken into account, and the new dreadnought class of battleship meant a further increase in the already enormous expenditure. By 1910 Great Britain was spending almost as much on her navy as Germany, France and Russia combined, and more than all six great powers had spent in 1890 (**259**).

Naval building and imperialism had become controversial subjects in Britain by 1900, and the debate over the Anglo-Boer war had divided the Liberal party into distinct factions. Public controversy over the course of foreign policy was not a new feature of British political life, however, and foreign observers had noted throughout the nineteenth century the extent to which the British parliamentary system encouraged division and debate. The government was required to inform, explain and defend its foreign policy to members of parliament – but whether this was a source of strength or weakness in the making of policy, or a factor encouraging isolation rather than commitment, is very difficult to judge. Most members of parliament believed that they must conduct themselves cautiously and responsibly when it came to questions of foreign policy, that the foreign secretary and his advisers had access to better sources of information than they, and that the public would disapprove if criticism weakened the government's ability to negotiate successfully.

Ironically then, while there was more open discussion and criticism of foreign policy in Britain than anywhere but France, there was also more continuity and coherence. Changes in government seldom meant dramatic changes in policy, and the government could usually be quite certain that it could mobilise the nation to support its policies. This coherence was due in large part to the widespread acceptance, among Britain's ruling classes, of certain basic assumptions that were to guide British relations with Europe. Arguments usually focused on methods, on questions of administration and organisation; the principles of the balance of power, of a strong navy, and of avoiding commitments that would draw Britain into a European war were generally adopted by both political parties and most politicians. A century of unparalleled power and prosperity had furnished convincing evidence that adherence to these principles ought to be maintained.

The Napoleonic wars had clarified the dangers with which Britain would be faced should one state succeed in establishing hegemony in Europe. Britain's economy had been severely disrupted by the interruption of trade with her best markets, which were always in Europe, and through the necessity of spending enormous sums on defence. Furthermore, there was little question that, had Napoleon succeeded in establishing real dominance and bending the whole of the European economy to suit the needs of France, he would eventually have been able to mount an effective challenge to Britain's overseas possessions, especially in India. No responsible Englishman believed that Britain could survive as a great power if Europe came under the control of France.

The balance of power was an idea that was rooted in the eighteenth-century enlightenment, and especially in the Newtonian concept of the physical universe. Ideally, the balance of forces among both heavenly bodies and states would regulate itself; but in the heavens divine intervention was sometimes necessary, as was occasional British intervention in European politics. The experience of the Napoleonic wars furnished another lesson here: for British intervention to succeed she needed to find one or more European allies – she was not able by herself to defeat a continental power that possessed a great army. For the balance of power to work, therefore, Britain had to assume that one or more European states would always find it in their interest to counterbalance the power of the strongest on their own if possible, with the assistance of Britain if necessary.

British policy in the forty years after the Congress of Vienna demonstrated this adherence to the principle of the balance. France, once she accepted her 'historical' frontiers and rejected the notion of a 'universal monarchy', became, in British eyes, a respectable member of the European system once again. The danger to the balance was now thought to come from Russia, which seemed to be in a position to dominate both eastern Europe, as her intervention in Hungary in 1848 demonstrated, and the near east, as her policy in the crisis leading up to the Crimean War in 1854 seemed to show. Russia was transformed into an enemy, France into an ally.

The Crimean War has become such a byword for incompetence that it is often forgotten that it was the only successful invasion of Russia in modern times. Britain achieved her basic aims: the Ottoman empire remained independent and relied more heavily on the advice of Britain than Russia; and the Habsburg empire was saved from declining to the level of a Russian satellite. The balance of power in Europe was maintained, but at the price of deeply-rooted Russian animosity. For the next half-century everyone expected a great Anglo-Russian war, particularly as the Russians undertook to balance the British threat to them in the Black Sea by posing a counter threat to the British empire in India. British foreign and defence policies for the next thirty years were devoted primarily to forestalling this Russian threat (**98**).

Partly for this reason, few Englishmen regarded the rise of Prussia and the creation of Germany as alarming. If anything, a strong German state seemed perfectly suited to the maintenance of the balance of power, situated as it was between France and Russia. Moreover, unlike France and Russia, Germany had no overseas interests and was unlikely to challenge either Britain's empire or her maritime supremacy. As long as Bismarck was satisfied with the post-1871 status quo in Europe, Germany was a 'natural' ally of Britain. The only undercurrent of concern came about as a result of Germany's dramatic victory in 1871. Britain began to worry that German power might be so great as to render France subordinate in the future: another Franco-German war might bring about the end of France as an independent state. This thinking led the British to warn Berlin during the 'Is War in Sight' crisis of 1875 that they would not permit such a war to take place (**128**).

Continuing Anglo-Russian antagonism and the revival of French imperialism in the 1870s worked to draw Britain closer to Germany and the Triple Alliance, and to diminish British worries about a possible German bid for hegemony. The Great Eastern crisis of 1878 and the Penjdeh crisis of 1886 convinced the British that the Russians still aimed to dominate the near east and to place themselves in a position to threaten an invasion of India. Britain's occupation of Egypt in 1881 struck a blow to French pride and led to a series of bitter quarrels in Asia and Africa. As long as France and Russia faced the might of the Triple Alliance in Europe, however, they were not likely to risk a conflict with Britain. In this way the balance of power contributed decisively to the defence of the British empire. And, as Russia and France appeared to be the restless, aggressive powers, determined to expand beyond Europe and to alter the balance within it, the British contributed to the stability of the Triple Alliance by assuring Italy and Austria-Hungary of their co-operation in the Mediterranean Agreements of 1886 and 1887 (**257**).

This state of affairs became less straightforward when Wilhelm II launched Germany on her 'new course' in foreign policy (**66**). She too now appeared to have an interest in overseas expansion, and a series of minor Anglo-German disputes arose over places like Samoa, Togoland and the Cameroons. The British government never took these disputes very seriously, but the kaiser's support for the Boers in South Africa and his decision of 1898 to build a fleet began to stimulate some opposition to the policy of co-operation with Germany. Throughout the 1890s, the Germans had attempted to draw the British into becoming full members of the Triple Alliance, but their entreaties had always been rejected, not because of germanophobia or the German bid for colonies, but because the British feared being drawn into a war in Europe for the sake of German interests. Thus, when the war broke out in South Africa, the Germans began to talk of a 'continental league' aimed at the British empire (**255**).

By 1900, therefore, the British found themselves isolated. Their traditional enemies, France and Russia, were allied with one another and had recently altered the terms of the alliance to provide for mutual action against the British. Their 'natural' ally, Germany, was increasingly antagonistic and apparently determined to cause them trouble wherever and whenever possible. The Anglo-Boer war demonstrated that this isolation posed little danger to the empire. The 'continental league' failed, and no joint action of the European powers was carried out; in fact, no action of any kind was taken against the British, who were able to fight the war in South Africa without worry of the consequences in the far east, central Asia and the Mediterranean. The empire was never in serious danger in the decades before 1914. The revolution in British diplomacy was sparked not by any immediate fear of a threat to the empire, but by concern for the European balance of power (**251, 258, 262**).

Part Three: The European Crisis

5 The Diplomatic Revolution

Viewed from a lofty perspective, the condition of European politics appears to have been unusually stable in 1900. The continent was clearly divided into two rival alliance systems: the Triple Alliance of Germany, Austria-Hungary and Italy; the Dual Alliance of France and Russia. Everyone who engaged in diplomatic and military affairs regarded the two alliances as the primary characteristic of international relations, and every question that arose in the years 1900–14 was assessed for its possible influence upon the alliance system. After 1914 many observers argued that the rival alliances made war inevitable, that any crisis was capable of leading all of the great powers into war, rather than being limited to a conflict between two or three of them. Most contemporaries, however, believed that, as the alliances were defensive, they bolstered the principle of the balance of power, which was the best guarantee of peace. As long as neither side enjoyed a clear superiority over the other, they argued, no statesman would risk the destruction of modern war and possible social upheaval. Both arguments, that the alliances made war inevitable, or that they made the chances of it remote, proved false.

The apparent stability of the alliances is deceptive. We know now that they endured, that the pattern of the central European powers opposed by France and Russia that emerged in the 1890s was the same basic pattern of conflict in the First World War. Yet there were some significant changes. Italy, a member of the Triple Alliance for more than thirty years, went to war against her former allies; Britain, independent of the alliance system in 1900 – and, if anything, enjoying better relations with the Triple Alliance – joined France and Russia to fight in 1914. Nor was it certain that the alliances would remain intact. French interests and ambitions in north Africa were never supported by Russia, and it was doubtful whether Russia would support France in a war with Italy, Britain or Germany that began over Tunis, Egypt or Morocco; it was equally doubtful whether France would fight to support Russia in Manchuria or Korea. The Triple Alliance sometimes appeared to be coming apart at the seams: Italy could always be tempted to turn against Austria-Hungary if France offered her concessions; Austria-Hungary had no interest in supporting Germany's *Weltpolitik* ('world policy') in central and southern Africa, in China and the Pacific; some Germans argued that it was a mistake to support Austria-Hungary in the Balkans, that it was preferable to restore good relations with Russia and thereby disrupt the Franco-Russian alliance.

The alliance system appears in retrospect to have been more stable than it actually was. Significant changes took place between 1900 and 1914; diplomats frequently questioned the usefulness of the arrangements; each side worked to dismantle the foundations upon which the rival alliance had been built. Nevertheless, the broad outlines of the system remained intact because the basic preoccupations of the great powers – their ambitions and their fears – survived the criticisms and the crises of the period from 1900 to 1914.

As the Triple Alliance and the Dual Alliance alike had been constructed entirely for European reasons, it should come as no surprise that complications beyond the frontiers of western and eastern Europe made it difficult for them to operate cohesively. This was certainly true in the far east, where, in the summer of 1900, a revolt that had been simmering in China for two years broke out in earnest. The 'Boxers' ('League of Righteous and Harmonious Fists'), with the tacit support of the dowager empress, murdered Christian missionaries in an anti-European campaign, marched upon Peking and besieged the foreign legation there. On 21 June 1900 the Chinese government declared war on the foreign powers, and it looked for a moment as if a great war would be waged in China that might result in her dismemberment.

Germany particularly feared the possible consequences of the Boxer rising. Wilhelm II had committed himself to an active role in the far east in 1897 when, in declaring that Germany was now a 'world power', he had seized the port of Tsingtao in Shantung province (**173**). If the rising led to a partition of China, German interests in China's future were likely to be forestalled, as Russia, Britain and Japan had much stronger forces in the area. The Germans therefore proposed to the British that they should uphold the principle of the 'open door' in China and maintain the integrity of the Chinese empire. The British, who had no desire to transform their sphere of influence in the Yangtse valley into a protectorate, agreed, hoping that co-operation with Germany would prevent the Russians from seizing Manchuria, which they had occupied during the Boxer crisis. The Anglo-German agreement on China was duly signed on 16 October 1900.

British hopes of using Germany's friendship to forestall Russian expansion in China soon vanished. When the Russians refused to evacuate Manchuria, the German chancellor, Bernhard von Bülow, announced that the agreement with Britain was not intended to apply to Manchuria. In other words, the Germans were not prepared to risk a crisis with Russia in Europe for the sake of their slight interests in the far east (**167**). The British, embroiled in a colonial war in South Africa, had already committed the bulk of their naval power and were in no position to forestall Russia on their own. They showed some interest, therefore, when, in March 1901, the Japanese approached them with the suggestion that they would be prepared to oppose Russia in Manchuria if the British, in exchange, could keep France neutral. The Japanese, who were determined to have Korea for themselves, believed that they could fight the Russians successfully if they did not have to face the combined fleets of Russia and France when attempting to land troops on the Chinese mainland.

An alliance with Japan offered some advantage to Britain, but this was not so clear-cut as it appears in retrospect (**276**). The British, in 1901, did not believe that Japan was strong enough to fight Russia, even if France were neutralised. In November and December of 1901 therefore, the British foreign secretary, Lord Lansdowne, revived the idea of an alliance with Germany; but the Germans demanded too high a price: Britain must join the Triple Alliance (**271**). Simultaneously, the Japanese were negotiating with the Russians on the basis of 'Man-Kan Kokan' – Japan to take Korea, Russia to take Manchuria (**89**). Because they could not prevent Russian expansion on their own, because German assistance depended on committing themselves to fighting France and Russia in Europe, and because a Russo-Japanese partition of China was the least desirable outcome of the crisis in the far east, the British chose to sign, on 30 January 1902, an alliance with Japan [**doc. 9**].

The Anglo-Japanese alliance did not make war more likely: the Japanese believed that it would strengthen their bargaining position by making it clear to Russia that she would be forced to fight without an ally, should it come to war. But the men making the decisions in Russia were not in a cautious mood. Military adventurers, admirals and some speculators, arguing that Russia's future lay in far eastern expansion, caught the ear of the tsar and stiffened his inclination not to compromise with the racially inferior Japanese. Moderates like the foreign minister, Count Lambsdorff, and the finance minister, Count Witte, were neglected in favour of the 'Korean' extremists, Bezobrazov, who was made a secretary of state, and Admiral Alexeiev, who was made viceroy of the far east. The Russian response to the Anglo-Japanese alliance was a new agreement with France. On 20 March 1902 a joint declaration was issued announcing, in effect, that the two would co-operate if a third party (Japan) threatened their interests by endangering China's integrity. It was quite evident that Russia was not going to back down without a fight.

The prospect of being drawn into a war against Britain for the sake of Russian interests in Manchuria and Korea was not a pleasant one for the French to contemplate (**110**). Their alliance with Russia had originally been designed exclusively for European purposes, to check Germany and the Triple Alliance. Ironically, after the Fashoda crisis demonstrated the failure of the alliance to operate outside Europe – Russia refusing any support against Britain – the French had proposed an expansion of its terms, and these were incorporated into the alliance in 1899. But the new terms, which provided for war with Britain, were designed by the French foreign minister, Delcassé, to encourage the British to negotiate over Egypt and Morocco; they were not supposed to draw France into a war.

Delcassé had no choice but to agree to Russia's insistence upon the joint declaration of March 1899 (**125**). Without the Russian alliance France would immediately be reduced to the level of a German subordinate in Europe, while there would be no hope of coercing the British into an agreement on north Africa. French policy, while it was guided by Delcassé from 1898 to 1905, was skilful and consistent, in contrast with the period 1871–90, when thirteen different foreign ministers had presided over policy. He believed that French power and prestige could be re-established by creating the great north African empire demanded by the *Comité de l'Afrique Française*, and he moved towards this first by seeking the assistance of Germany, then by expanding the terms of the Dual Alliance (**247**). But there was a third possibility: perhaps the British themselves would consent to a colonial settlement without coercion (**225**).

Events beyond the control of the diplomats produced the agenda of diplomacy. In the midst of the far eastern crisis, Morocco appeared to be falling apart of its own accord. Tribes hostile to the Sultan of Morocco revolted against his authority in late 1902 and he seemed powerless to stop them. Britain and France alike feared the consequences of an uncontrolled revolt – Britain because it might threaten Gibraltar, France because it might threaten Algeria – and both turned to Germany for diplomatic support. Germany, who always saw Anglo-French quarrels as working to her advantage, turned them both down. Hoping to promote a crisis, the Germans unwittingly encouraged an Anglo-French entente.

The improvement in Anglo-French relations was symbolised by the visit of King Edward VII to Paris in May 1903, and the return visit of President Loubet and Delcassé to London in July. The negotiations for a settlement of colonial differences, which began in earnest in the summer of 1903, were thus surrounded by an aura of public goodwill – a sentimental factor that assisted the diplomats in their endeavours, but was certainly not the primary cause of the eventual settlement (**95**).

The French would have found it more difficult to pursue a settlement with Britain if the Russians had strenuously objected, but they did not. Partly this was the result of misplaced confidence in Russia's strength in the far east: the 'Koreans' argued that they could defeat the Japanese without French assistance if the British did not intervene, an argument that was strengthened by the opening of the trans-Siberian railway in August 1903. Equally important, the tsar and his military advisers had decided in 1901 and 1902 that the continued existence of France as a great power was vital to Russian security in Europe. In March 1901 they concluded that France could not survive a war with Germany unless Russia mobilised rapidly and attacked Germany in the east; this led to a new mobilisation scheme, 'Plan 18', which was formally approved in November 1902. The Russian commitment to France remained firm. The Dual Alliance, which had failed to apply to Russia's benefit in the far east or to France's benefit in Africa, remained the most essential element in the European policy of each power.

When Japan attacked Russia at Port Arthur on 8 February 1904, therefore, it had little immediate impact upon power politics in Europe; it disrupted neither the Dual Alliance nor the Anglo-French colonial discussions (**101**). If anything, the Japanese attack encouraged France and Britain to reach an agreement. In spite of the success of the attack, no one yet anticipated a Japanese victory even though they enjoyed a naval superiority and their army outnumbered the Russian army of the far east by 330,000 to 100,000.

Thus the discussions between Britain and France continued and were even hurried along. The agreement, signed on 8 April 1904, resolved a variety of outstanding differences in Newfoundland, Gambia, Nigeria, Madagascar, Siam and the New Hebrides (**260**). But the essence of the agreement lay in the provisions pertaining to Egypt and Morocco. What the British wanted in Egypt was an end to the troublesome opposition of France, both on Egypt's frontiers and within the committee of bondholders who were responsible for Egypt's financial affairs. Such a promise from France would reduce the expense involved in safeguarding Egypt and make it possible to continue with financial reform more quickly and more easily. In return the French wanted Britain to acknowledge their primacy in Morocco. In a secret protocol to the agreement, Britain promised the French that, should the sultan's authority in Morocco disappear, she would give them a free hand in Morocco – providing the coastline opposite Gibraltar went to Spain and that this strip of territory would remain unfortified. The French, in other words, finally recognised the permanence of the British occupation of Egypt in exchange for the freedom to establish their own occupation of Morocco.

The Anglo-French entente was nothing like an alliance. No enemy was singled out. No contingencies were provided for. No joint actions were planned. The entente was simply a settlement of colonial disputes that had been simmering for the last quarter-century. Such a scheme had surfaced repeatedly during these years, but had never emerged successfully because of French intransigence on the Egyptian question. France, in fact, conceded little in Egypt: the British occupation had become stable and, under Cromer's guiding hand, progressive. What the French gave up was a dream. And herein lies the true significance of the entente. Anglo-French antagonism had been one of the steady factors upon which European diplomats and strategists had come to rely. The end of the antagonism was bound to cause reverberations throughout the system. No one at the time imagined that this would end with millions of British troops fighting a war in Europe alongside France (**235**).

The Anglo-French entente did not signify a diplomatic revolution; it did no more than suggest that one might be possible. But there were other suggestions of this at the same time. In the midst of the entente negotiations Russia and Austria-Hungary agreed, at

Murzsteg in October 1903, to co-operate in preventing disturbances in Macedonia from undermining the peace in the Balkans. The possibility that the crisis in the far east might cause fundamental shifts in Russia's European policy began to be considered. Perhaps the commitment to expansion and war in Asia would lead the Russians to welcome a revived *Dreikaiserbund*; perhaps the failure of the French to support their ally would lead the Russians to abandon the alliance. The Germans encouraged these ideas and pushed them further along when they signed a new commercial treaty with Russia in July 1904.

When ships in Russia's Baltic fleet, steaming to join the fighting in the far east, mistook some British fishing boats for Japanese warships and fired upon them off the Dogger Bank, the stage seemed set for a major shift in European diplomacy. Germany proposed an alliance to Russia. They were to promise one another assistance against attack by 'a European power' – i.e., Germany would aid Russia against Britain, Russia would aid Germany against France. The Germans even proposed that the Franco-Russian alliance be maintained, as they imagined that it provided for war against Britain, as well as Germany. However, the Russians, in November 1904, refused the offer. There was to be no Russo-German equivalent of the Anglo-French entente.

The Germans, in spite of the apparently cautious terms they had suggested, were asking too high a price and had too little to offer in return. There were no Gambias or Madagascars in Russo-German relations. Even the idea of assistance against Britain could not be taken seriously. The German army was of no use against the empire, the German navy was in no condition to challenge the British, and some Germans even feared that the British would launch a preventive attack, destroying the German warships in harbour before they were strong enough to defend themselves (**179**). The Germans could offer the Russians little more than safety on their western frontier. But Bülow and Wilhelm II would not be satisfied with a simple revival of the old *Dreikaiserbund*, for this would have been an admission of failure, a demonstration that the *Neue Kurs* had failed and that Bismarck had been right all along.

Any arrangement with Russia had to emphasise Germany's strength and the success of Bülow's 'world policy' (**128, 168**). What the Germans were proposing was a 'continental league' with Germany at the centre, directing Russia and France – neither of whom were able to stand alone, or even, as the war with Japan had shown, together. But the negotiations in the autumn of 1904 showed that Russia did not feel herself to be so weak as to compel her to join Germany. When the negotiations failed, Bülow, and the head of the political section in the German foreign ministry, Friedrich von Holstein, decided that they might be more successful in persuading the weaker member of the Dual Alliance, France, into joining Germany. Bülow and Holstein were also anxious to show the French that their entente with the British was of little use to them when it came to relations with Germany.

An opportunity almost exactly designed to fit German specifications came in January 1905 when a French mission' arrived at Fez, the capital of Morocco, with the aim of making clear France's paramount position there by insisting upon a programme of internal reform (**63, 245**). The Germans knew how deeply the French were committed to their ambitions in Morocco, for practically the entire French foreign ministry, and especially the bureaucrats of the Quai d'Orsay, aspired to establish a French empire there. When the sultan appealed to the Germans for assistance, therefore, they readily complied. On 31 March a somewhat reluctant Wilhelm II, about to embark upon a Mediterranean cruise, landed at Tangier with his entourage and rode through the streets in military uniform on a magnificent horse, with a band playing. When he reached the German legation he declared that he would support the continued independence of the Moroccan state. Germany, he announced, knew how to safeguard her interests.

But it was the very absence of German interests that gave this, the first Moroccan crisis, its peculiar character. The French had frequently approached the Germans over the previous decade with proposals for an arrangement over Morocco; Delcassé in particular believed that German assistance might be useful there in the contest with Great Britain. The Germans always replied that they lacked sufficient interests there to become embroiled in a dispute (**153**). Now they were suddenly reversing their position. The point of the crisis, however, was not Morocco, but the nature of the relationship between Germany and France. If, in an area where France had great interests and ambitions while Germany had none, the French were forced to give in to German demands, it would make it plain that Germany was so much more powerful in Europe that France could have an empire overseas only with Germany's consent (**115**). It would not matter that the French navy was more powerful, that French forces in the area were stronger – all that mattered was Germany's ability to defeat France in Europe. The Moroccan crisis was so significant because it seemed likely to determine whether or not France was still capable of pursuing an independent foreign policy.

It was this question of French independence that drew the British into the crisis. Over the past decade a group of young men had arisen within the British foreign office who were convinced that Germany posed a greater threat to the British empire than either Russia or France – a threat that was symbolised by the German decision to build a great fleet. They argued that it was only the existence of France and Russia that kept German ambitions in check. These men, led by Francis Bertie, Arthur Nicolson, Charles Hardinge and Eyre Crowe, had, by the time of the first Moroccan crisis, achieved positions of authority. They were now convinced that if the French were forced to back down it would be but the first step towards France becoming a satellite of Germany; in order to prevent this they argued that Britain must find some way to steady French nerves. They did not suggest that the entente had imposed this necessity on Britain; rather, it was precisely because the entente was *not* an alliance that they had to find some new way of reassuring the French.

The foreign secretary, Lord Lansdowne, in May 1905 assured the French ambassador in London, Paul Cambon, that Britain was prepared to transform the entente into an alliance. Lansdowne's words were vague but encouraging, as he suggested that Britain and France should 'discuss in advance any contingencies by which they might in the course of events find themselves confronted' (**116**). In Paris, Delcassé argued that these words were the prelude to an alliance. But his prime minister, Rouvier, believed that a crisis might lead to war with Germany and to the certain defeat of France. Hints of British assistance were not enough: even if such aid were forthcoming, the British navy 'does not run on wheels'. When the Germans demanded that Delcassé be forced to resign at the end of May, therefore, Rouvier agreed. The Germans thereby scored a great diplomatic victory: the architect of the Anglo-French entente had been forced out of office due to German pressure, and it appeared that France was no longer able to pursue a foreign policy independent of German wishes. The kaiser made von Bülow a prince, and Rouvier consented to Germany's demand for an international conference to settle the Moroccan issue.

Germany's success in Morocco was underscored by Russia's

defeat in the far east. After a long and slow voyage from Europe, the Russian Baltic fleet had finally arrived off the coast of Japan in May 1905, where it was almost immediately destroyed. The battle of Tsushima on 27 May 1905 left Japan in absolute control of the sea. The Germans quickly renewed the alliance discussions that had failed the previous November. On 24 July the kaiser met the tsar at Björkö and persuaded him to sign a defensive alliance with Germany. The success of the new course and world policy seemed guaranteed: French ambitions had been checked in Morocco, Russian strength sapped in the far east; both would submit to German-directed alliances and Britain would be isolated.

Within three months of the meeting at Björkö it became plain that the German victory was less than clear-cut. First, the tsar's closest advisers, the Grand Duke Nicholas Nikolayevich, Count Witte and Count Lambsdorff (the foreign minister), all advised against a German alliance, insisting that it would represent an abandonment of France, mean the end of the balance of power in Europe and the encouragement of German designs in the near east. It was apparent to his advisers, if not to Nicholas II himself, that the apparently 'defensive' arrangement would reduce Russia to dependence on Germany. The treaty of Björkö was therefore rejected in November. Secondly, the British decided that they would have to go further than Lansdowne's vague indications of support if the French will to resist German demands was to be bolstered. In December 1905 secret discussions with the French general staff were initiated in order to consider joint operations in the event of war (**102**). The British had implicitly recognised the validity of Rouvier's earlier point: they would have to hold out the prospect of military assistance in order to bolster the French.

By the time the Morocco conference met at Algeçiras in southern Spain on 16 January 1906 Germany's position had been weakened considerably. Russia had chosen the Dual Alliance rather than the Björkö agreement; France had agreed on a division of Morocco with Spain; and the new British foreign secretary, Sir Edward Grey, quickly showed that he was more suspicious of Germany and therefore more inclined to support France than Lansdowne had been (**127**). Germany could not even count on her allies. The Italians, in December 1900, had secretly pledged to recognise the special interests of France in Morocco in exchange for a similar recognition of their rights in Libya. Then, on 30 June 1902 two days after the Triple Alliance had been renewed, the Italian foreign minister, Giulio Prinetti, signed a secret agreement with the French ambassador, Camille Barrère, that pledged Italy to remain neutral in any conflict into which France had been provoked. Prince von Bülow recognised, shortly after the conference convened, that Germany could not hope for a successful outcome: the only power sympathetic to her was Austria-Hungary – and even she counselled moderation. The final act of the conference, signed on 7 April 1906, although it affirmed Morocco's independence and integrity, left the policing of the country to France and Spain and gave the control of the *Banque d'Etat* to France, thereby leaving her in control of Morocco's economic development (**72, 194**).

The Moroccan *débacle* had immediate repercussions within Germany. Holstein, the grey eminence of the foreign office who had done much to engineer German policy, was forced to resign (**161**). General von Möltke, who succeeded Schlieffen as chief of the general staff in January, proposed to alter the war-plan against France by providing for a pre-emptive strike through Belgium (**159**). Admiral von Tirpitz, whose fleet-building scheme had been challenged in the autumn of 1905 by the British decision to begin constructing the huge new 'dreadnought' class of battleship, was now able to get the approval of the Reichstag for an accelerated building programme of bigger ships in the Third Navy Law, which was ratified on 5 June 1906. A more general effect of the Moroccan crisis inside Germany was the widespread impression that she was being 'encircled', that the other European states resented her growing power and prosperity and would do everything they could to prevent Germany from assuming her rightful place as a world power. Germany, her leaders concluded, must rely less upon diplomacy and more upon her own military and naval strength.

There certainly seemed to be evidence to support the German belief that the ring around them was drawing tighter. Barely two weeks after the Algeçiras Act was signed the Russians agreed to a French proposal that the clauses in the Dual Alliance providing for military co-operation in a war against Great Britain should now be dropped. The French themselves had proposed these clauses in the aftermath of the Fashoda crisis; to drop them now indicated that they no longer regarded Britain as a possible enemy. This was still some distance from an alliance with Britain, but it is signifi-cant nevertheless because German policy since the accession of Wilhelm II had been predicated upon the assumption that Anglo-French and Anglo-Russian rivalry overseas would become increasingly bitter, and that this would work to Germany's benefit. Instead, the three powers showed signs that they might draw closer together: on 17 April France provided a huge new loan of 2,250,000,000 francs to Russia to shore up her disintegrating finances in the wake of the war against Japan; in 1905 the British government decided to transfer ships from the Mediterranean – where they were deployed to guard against France and Russia – to the North Sea in order to meet the growing challenge from Germany (**274**). The question that remained was whether or not Britain and Russia would also find a way to resolve their differences (**239**).

In the midst of the Moroccan crisis any reconciliation of Britain and Russia seemed most unlikely. On 12 August 1905 Britain and Japan had agreed upon a revision of their alliance that extended its terms considerably and in a way highly unfavourable to Russia. First, it was extended geographically to include India and adjacent territories: the Japanese would now be required to assist Britain if Russia attacked in central Asia. Secondly, the alliance would now operate if Russia attacked on her own: the provision for a two-power attack was dropped, so Russia, even without French assistance, would face combined British and Japanese forces should she become embroiled in a war with either of them.

The Russian failure in the far east, however, might render the revised Anglo-Japanese alliance insignificant. If Russia now decided to pursue a policy of caution in her relations with Britain and Japan, the new terms might never come into operation; and caution was made more likely by the moderate conditions of the Treaty of Portsmouth, which ended the Russo-Japanese war on 5 September 1905. In essence, all the treaty provided for was a Russian recognition of Japanese predominance in Korea and the withdrawal of Russian forces from southern Manchuria and south Sakhalin. These were hardly oppressive terms: there was no indemnity, and the Japanese public was far more disappointed than the Russian with the conditions of peace. There was no popular cry for revenge in Russia, no stimulus to further adventure. The 'Koreans', the 'Easterners' or the 'Asiatics' in Russian governing circles had, in fact, been discredited. And, as the men in these circles had been generally 'pro-German', arguing that good relations with Germany on the western frontier gave Russia the safety necessary to expand in the east and central Asia, the pro-German line of policy also suffered a setback. Finally, the disasters of the war had led to chaos and rebellion at home – the most famous incident of which was the 'Bloody Sunday' of 22 January 1905 when the troops of the tsar fired upon a peaceful demonstration, killing hundreds. Not only did this discontent provide further impetus for a policy of restraint, it led to the signing of the October Manifesto on 30 October 1905, in which the tsar promised new civil rights, a representative assembly (*Duma*) and a constitution. These promises were given effect in the 'Fundamental Laws' of 6 May 1905. Although the new system was far different from that of a parliamentary democracy, it did encourage the formation and circulation of public opinion; and most of this opinion, in the decade that followed, was unhappy with the idea of further adventures in central and eastern Asia (**222**).

The new Russian foreign minister, A. P. Izvolsky, came into office in May 1906 eager to limit Russian commitments and to put relations with all the great powers on a more equable footing. Over the next seventeen months he managed to reach a political agreement with Japan (recognising her authority in Korea and southern Manchuria in exchange for her recognition of Russian authority in northern Manchuria and outer Mongolia), an agreement with Germany to maintain the status quo in the Baltic, and an agreement with Britain on Persia and Afghanistan. Izvolsky did not seek an alliance with Britain; he did not aim to 'encircle' Germany. Rather, his policy aimed to provide stability and calm in Russia's foreign relations while the new political system took root and time healed the damage done by the Japanese war. The Anglo-Russian entente, which was signed on 31 August 1907, was even less of a political partnership than the Anglo-French entente had been (**70**). The two powers agreed that Tibet should act as a neutral buffer between their empires and that Russia should have no direct contact with Afghanistan. Thus, the British seemed to have achieved the security for their north-west frontier that they had long sought. Most difficult, and most important, was the agreement on Persia, which created a Russian sphere of influence in the more populous and richer north, and a British sphere in the south, bordering on Afghanistan and the Persian Gulf; a neutral sphere in the centre was to separate the two (**260**).

Like the Anglo-French entente, the Anglo-Russian provided for no political action, no military planning and suggested no possible contingencies that might lead the two powers to consult on these matters in the future. It was a simple resolution – and by no means a complete one – of long-standing differences that had made for troubled relations in central Asia (**114**, **253**). Like the Anglo-

French entente, however, even this cautious arrangement jeopardised German strategy, which had assumed that Britain and Russia
would remain enemies and that this would eventually take one or
the other of them into the German camp as a subordinate ally
(**138, 154**).

6 The Vortex of South-eastern Europe

With the Anglo-Japanese alliance and the Russo-Japanese political agreement in the far east, with the Anglo-French entente resolving differences in the Pacific, in North America, south-east Asia and Africa, and with the Anglo-Russian entente resolving differences in central Asia, it is not surprising that most diplomatic disputes in the following years were located in, or near, Europe itself. This is not to suggest that Great Britain had carefully crafted a series of arrangements with old rivals in order to enable her to prepare for the inevitable conflict with imperial Germany. While it is true that some British officials felt threatened by German pretensions to world power, it is also true that practically nothing was done to transform the colonial ententes into European alliances. Moreover, the Russians, while they believed that the continued existence of France as an independent great power was essential to the balance of power and thus vital to their own security, did not believe that Germany posed any immediate danger to them. The 'diplomatic revolution' of 1904–07 thus represented a shift in mood and a change in emphasis: it did not represent the forging of a coalition that made war predictable.

Many of those who participated in the diplomatic process believed that the balance of power that had been created with the establishment of the rival alliance systems was the best guarantee of peace, and it was certainly arguable that the alliances had provided stability within Europe, where there had not been a significant crisis since the Russo-Turkish war of 1878 (**81**). As important as the alliance system itself, however, was the agreement between Russia and Austria-Hungary in 1897 to put the Balkans 'on ice'. The co-operation between the two powers had been extended in 1903 when, with a crisis brewing in Macedonia, they had met at Murzsteg and agreed upon a programme of reforms that would preserve peace in the Balkans.

Ironically, this co-operation laid the groundwork for the first European crisis in thirty years. Following a confrontation between Vienna and Budapest over their respective rights within the Dual

Monarchy, a new foreign minister, Count Aehrenthal, came into office in 1906 determined to demonstrate that these internal diffi-culties did not mean the end of Austria-Hungary as a great power. More important still, he decided that some of the monarchy's prob-lems, especially those arising from questions of nationality, could actually be solved by a vigorous foreign policy (**198**). The new chief of the general staff, Baron Conrad, supported Aehrenthal's view that the troublesome Serbs of southern Hungary could be silenced by reducing the independence and the pretensions of Serbia. The first step in this design would be to annex Bosnia and Herzegovina, the two autonomous provinces of the Ottoman empire, inhabited mainly by Serbs, that had been administered by Austria-Hungary since 1878. The annexation would deny the Serb dream of a large Serbian state incorporating all Serbian people. The Russian foreign minister, Izvolsky, consented to this plan (**69, 193**).

Izvolsky's aim was partly to maintain the spirit of co-operation with the Austrians, partly to score a diplomatic triumph that would bolster Russia's flagging prestige without putting her in any danger. On 16 September 1908 Izvolsky met Aehrenthal at Büchlau in Moravia, where he became convinced that the Austrians intended to occupy the provinces and that it would be dangerous and foolhardy to oppose them. He proposed, instead, that in exchange for Russia's consent to the annexation, Austria-Hungary should support Russia's wish to have the Straits of the Bosphorus and the Dardanelles opened to the passage of warships in peacetime.

If the bargain had worked, Austro-Russian co-operation in the Balkans might have been maintained. But the Russian government refused to support Izvolsky, partly because public opinion, more important under the new constitutional process, would be enraged by the abandonment of Slav brothers to Germanic rule. Izvolsky himself insisted that the Austrians had violated a number of the promises they had made at Büchlau. On the other hand, the Austrians, led by the bellicose Conrad, were prepared to fight, while the Russians were not. The Germans gave their complete support for Austria's policy, while the French and the British were not willing to act on Russia's behalf (**104**). When, in February 1904, the Austrians demanded that Russia and Serbia recognise the annexation or prepare for the invasion of Serbia, the Russians felt that they had no choice but to comply. What had begun in the spirit of co-operation ended in bitterness and suspicion (**192**).

The Bosnian crisis was a turning-point in several significant ways (**134**). First, it killed the Austro-Russian co-operation that had kept the Balkans reasonably quiet for the previous thirty years; from this point on the Balkans were in an almost constant state of turmoil. Secondly, it convinced Serbia that Austria-Hungary was aiming at her destruction as an independent state; from now on Serbian nationalists believed that they must rely on Russia for support and that, ultimately, only the break-up of the Dual Monarchy could save them. Finally, and most important, the Russians concluded that the Austro-German unity during the crisis posed a direct threat to them. Contrary to their decisions following the war with Japan, they did not abandon the Balkans or come to an agreement with their antagonist. The Balkans and the Straits, they believed, were vital to their security, to their reputation as a great power, and to their internal harmony. They strengthened their ties with Serbia, refurbished their mobilisation plans, and undertook a campaign of battleship building in the Black Sea.

The new Russian foreign minister, S. D. Sazonov, who replaced Izvolsky in September 1910, seems to have decided that, apart from strengthening the Russian presence in the Balkans, the best method of countering Austria-Hungary was to drive a wedge between her and Germany. His first visit was to Potsdam where he agreed to drop Russian objections to German enterprises in the Ottoman empire and Persia in exchange for a German promise not to support aggressive Austrian moves in the Balkans. The conclusion drawn by the Germans from the Bosnian crisis was that neither the alliance with France nor the entente with Britain provided Russia with the assistance she required in the Balkans (**265**).

The Germans were tempted into believing that they could apply the same logic in their relations with France, when, in the spring of 1911, more trouble broke out in Morocco (**65**). Demonstrators rioting in Fez against the rule of the sultan encouraged French colonialists to believe that the opportunity to impose French rule had come at last. In the French foreign ministry the colonial party was firmly in control of policy: a weak minister, Jean Cruppi, who was ignorant of foreign affairs and incapable of countering their arguments for intervention, ordered troops to Morocco on 17 April. By 21 May a joint Franco-Moroccan force of 20,000 had occupied Fez (**62**).

The French move violated both the Algeciras Act of 1906, which left the Germans with some privileges in Morocco, and a Franco-

German agreement of 1909 that recognised France's special political interests in Morocco in exchange for a promise that Germany's economic interests would not be damaged. These legal niceties counted for little, but they did provide the Germans with a legitimate excuse for responding to the French move. On the other hand, the German foreign minister, Alfred von Kiderlen-Wächter, whose ultimatum to Russia had proven to be such a dramatic success in the Bosnian crisis, privately believed that Morocco was bound to fall to the French (**111**). He decided to act not in order to protect German interests but to demonstrate to the French that they were in no position to act unilaterally or to violate agreements with Germany. The French would have to offer concessions before he would recognise their authority in Morocco; precisely what these were mattered little and Kiderlen had not defined them. On 1 July 1911 a German gunboat, the *Panther*, steamed into the Moroccan port of Agadir, and a new Moroccan crisis began (**178**).

The British had not been pleased with the French decision to occupy Fez, which they interpreted as a triumph for the troublesome colonialists at the Quai d'Orsay. When the Germans sent the *Panther*, however, they quickly forgot their irritation with the French. The officials of the Foreign Office concluded that Germany was not attempting to secure concessions but to disrupt the entente by showing France that she was too weak to resist German demands; they feared that, without strong support from Britain, the French would be thrown into the 'teuton embrace' (**252, 261, 267**). Sir Edward Grey was more moderate. He was prepared to countenance French concessions to Germany in the Congo in return for French control of Morocco; but even he began to worry when it appeared that the Germans were demanding most of the French Congo. Nevertheless, the cabinet, fearing that a strong line might lead to war, instructed Grey to inform the French that they would not regard as a legitimate cause of war a French decision to resist German territorial gains in Morocco.

British actions during the crisis show that they, like the Germans, were not deeply concerned with Morocco or the Congo. What worried them was that German power in Europe could be used to control French behaviour overseas; if this proved to be the result of the crisis, then France would be reduced to subordinate status and the balance of power in Europe would have shifted clearly in Germany's favour. In other words, Britain had no immediate fear of German imperialism, but she did regard the balance of power as essential to her security and she was increasingly concerned that this was being endangered by Germany. This thinking was quite different from that which had led to the entente in 1904 and explains why, on 21 July 1911, the chancellor of the exchequer, David Lloyd George, gave a strong speech at the Mansion House warning that Britain was not to be ignored in such matters (**139, 266**). The Germans were offended, the British fleet was placed on alert and the crisis deepened.

The crisis was resolved in October and November by the French conceding to the Germans two strips of territory in the Congo (amounting to some 100,000 square miles) in exchange for a recognition of the French protectorate in Morocco. The resolution pleased no one. The French colonialists, who had initiated the crisis, felt they had been abandoned by the British and by their own politicians; but they were themselves soon discredited. Raymond Poincaré led a parliamentary inquiry into the handling of the crisis that condemned the power of the officials at the Quai d'Orsay, and within a few months he had become premier and foreign minister, determined to avoid colonial adventures and to work closely with Russia and Britain. Grey, and his less moderate officials, felt that French impetuosity had brought them to the brink of war; although he believed that France must be supported in the event of a conflict with Germany, he was determined to restrain French adventurism (**268**). In Germany, Kiderlen had succeeded neither in subordinating France nor in driving a wedge into the entente; even the Congo concessions did not help him to save face. Where he had succeeded in the Balkans he failed in Morocco, and the general impression drawn from the crisis was that it was the wicked British who were pulling the strings in their effort to encircle Germany and prevent her natural development into a world power.

The only ones truly satisfied with the crisis were the Italians. In a secret agreement signed in December 1900 they had recognised the special interests of France in Morocco in return for a French recognition of their special interests in the Ottoman provinces of Tripolitania and Cyrenaica (Libya). When the French moved into Fez the Italians began to consider a similar move into Tripoli. Public support for such a move was widespread and enthusiastic; the government, in fact, was more cautious than the people. But the Italians had also prepared the diplomatic ground more carefully than the French in Morocco: in March 1902 Britain had recognised Italy's special interests in Libya, and in October 1909

Russia had been persuaded to do the same; the Italians assumed that they could count on Germany and Austria-Hungary, their partners in the Triple Alliance, to support them. On 20 September the Italian government decided to invade Libya, believing that the war would be short and simple; as it turned out, the campaign lasted more than a year and formal recognition of the Italian annexation of Libya did not come until after the First World War (**199, 202, 208**).

Although no power opposed Italy's invasion of Libya, no one gave their enthusiastic support – least of all her partners in the Triple Alliance. The chief of the Austrian general staff proposed to take advantage of Italy's commitment in Africa by attacking her in the north – but this daring plan was rejected. What the powers feared was that the Italian invasion would have repercussions throughout the Ottoman empire. There was a growing belief in all the European capitals that the empire was in danger of dissolution, and that this would raise untold complications, as the near east was the one region where all six great powers had interests and ambitions (**64, 211, 243**).

The British in particular worried that this succession of crises in the Mediterranean would, if the pattern continued, lead to war. By 1911 one of the basic elements in the pattern was the Anglo-German naval race (**148**). It would be quite wrong to assume, however, that the British immediately interpreted the German decision to build a navy as a threat to the empire. In spite of the German naval bills of 1898 and 1900, the British government continued to calculate its naval requirements on the basis of the two-power standard of France and Russia (**175**). Only when the Russian fleet was destroyed by the Japanese did the Admiralty propose to substitute Germany for Russia in their calculation. Even then the change was not a political decision to view Germany as the coming enemy but was rather a continuation of the policy of being prepared to fight Britain's two strongest rivals, should they combine with one another. At the time of the first Moroccan crisis no one believed that Germany on her own would be able to match the British navy, and no one believed in a Franco-German alliance. The decisive change came when, in the midst of the Moroccan crisis, it was decided that Germany was aiming at hegemony in Europe, the first stage of which was the domination of France. Only then did Germany begin to be seen as Britain's principal rival, and this for continental political reasons, not imperial and naval ones (**177, 272**).

British planners began to construct contingency plans for war against Germany in 1905, long before the German fleet was seen as a serious threat to British security. The plans were conceived to assist France in the event of a German attack; and this was underlined when the Committee of Imperial Defence decided, during the Moroccan crisis, that an expeditionary force should be created that could assist France in fighting on the continent itself. From 1905 on, changes were instituted that were designed to meet the German threat: more of the fleet was concentrated in home waters, new battleship building paralleled that of Germany. By 1911 everyone spoke of the Anglo-German naval 'race' and some believed that it was the real cause of the antagonism between the two countries that brought them close to war during the Agadir crisis (**78**).

When the minister of war, Viscount Haldane, was sent on a special mission to Germany in February 1912, therefore, some members of the government hoped that an end to the naval race could be negotiated and that this would diminish the growing Anglo-German antagonism. But the mission failed. On the eve of his arrival, new and more ambitious navy and army bills were announced in the Reichstag; and, in the negotiations that followed the Germans insisted that the first step in any naval agreement must be a British promise of neutrality in the event of war (**132**). The German moves merely served to convince Sir Edward Grey that his fears were justified, that Germany wished to neutralise Britain in order to dominate France (**79**). He concluded that only strong British support for France would enable her to retain her independence, but he refused to turn this support into an alliance mainly out of fear that this would encourage French adventurism.

His fear was probably no longer justified after Poincaré, who aimed to subdue the adventurers in the Quai d'Orsay, became premier of France in January 1912. Poincaré believed that colonialists and revanchists had brought France to the brink of disaster in the Agadir crisis; he preferred a policy of caution and stability, and the best guarantee of stability, he believed, was to be found in the balance of power that had been established with the alliance system. France, he said, should be a firm and loyal ally of Russia, draw as close as possible to Britain and avoid the temptation of working to disrupt the Triple Alliance, either by an agreement with Italy or with Germany. This policy, apparently more cautious and straightforward, was potentially more dangerous in one respect: under Poincaré the French would no longer fail to support Russia

61

in the Balkans. In September 1912 he assured Izvolsky that if a crisis in the Balkans led Russia into a war with the Central Powers she could count on France fulfilling her obligations to her ally (**103, 215**).

Poincaré was relying largely upon Izvolsky's own predilection for a cautious policy when he made this commitment. But there were other, less cautious, forces at work within Russia and in the Balkans. The Italian war with Turkey had encouraged the Balkan states, particularly Serbia and Bulgaria, to anticipate the final dissolution of the Ottoman empire in Europe, which would make it possible for them to incorporate into their states the Serbs and Bulgars who remained in the Turkish province of Macedonia. Serbia and Bulgaria had long been antagonistic towards one another for various political and cultural reasons, but two Russian ambassadors, Hartwig in Serbia and Neklyudov in Bulgaria, urged them to forget their differences and come together in the spirit of Slavic brotherhood. In March 1912 a Serbo-Bulgarian alliance was signed (**119**). Within a few months a complicated network of alliances and alignments had been constructed linking Greece and Montenegro with Serbia and Bulgaria in a 'Balkan League' (**129**). In spite of the efforts of both Russia and Austria-Hungary to restrain them, the Montenegrins declared war on Turkey on 8 October 1912 and the other Balkan states quickly joined in. The Turks were defeated rather easily in the Balkans, although the Bulgarian attack on Constantinople became bogged down in the mud (**140, 218**).

The defeat of the Turks suited neither the Austrians nor the Russians. An expanded Serbia, with a coastline on the Adriatic, would prove an even more troublesome neighbour for Austria-Hungary, encouraging the growth of Serb nationalism within the Dual Monarchy. A big Bulgarian state in possession of Constantinople would be in a position to inflict serious damage on Russia, especially if she continued to work in conjunction with the Austrians. The two great powers informed the Balkan states, therefore, that no change in the status quo would be permitted without their consent, and a conference of ambassadors met in London in December 1912 to sort things out (**71**).

The general principle adopted at the conference was that the Turks should lose their remaining possessions in Europe, except for a rump of land around the Dardanelles and Bosphorous Straits stretching from Enos to Midia. This satisfied Russia. The conference also agreed that an independent state should be created in Albania. This satisfied Austria-Hungary because it limited Serbian gains to a restricted area in the interior. Both great powers had feared that the war would upset the balance in the Balkans and that potential enemies would be placed in a position to pose a much greater threat than hitherto; but diplomacy had proved to be sufficient, due to the reluctance of Russia and Austria-Hungary to champion the cause of Serbia and Bulgaria, and to the continuing rivalry among the Balkan states themselves. The 'preliminaries of peace' were signed in London on 31 May 1913 (**109**).

Within a month war had again broken out. The Bulgarians felt that they had been cheated of a proper victory in the First Balkan War because the Serbs and Greeks had occupied, and retained, territories that ought to have gone to Bulgaria. At the end of June, therefore, they attacked the Serbs, and the Second Balkan War was underway. The Greeks immediately joined in against the Bulgarians; so too did the Rumanians and the Turks. Bulgaria was easily defeated and by the end of July she was suing for peace. The Treaty of Bucharest, signed on 10 August 1913, expanded the territories of Serbia, Greece and Rumania; a further Treaty of Constantinople, signed on 30 September 1913, permitted Turkey to recover some of the territory she had earlier lost to Bulgaria (**82**).

The wars and their settlement left a dangerous legacy in the Balkans (**80**). The victors, bigger and more powerful, remained dissatisfied: Serbia, which had doubled in size, was still landlocked and made plain its sympathy with the Serbs of Austria-Hungary whom it regarded as oppressed brethren; Greece, which had expanded to take in almost all territories where Greek was the language of the majority, looked beyond her frontiers to a 'greater Greece' that included Constantinople and substantial portions of Asia Minor. Austria-Hungary and Turkey had good reason to believe that new dangers lay ahead. And Bulgaria, not surprisingly, was embittered by the disasters of the previous year – she had lost 25,000 men and been brought to the verge of revolution; she would eagerly grasp any situation that offered her an opportunity to reverse the verdict of 1913 (**197**).

The success of Russia's client, Serbia, might lead one to expect that the Russians would have been satisfied by the outcome of the wars, but two factors worked against this. First, at decisive moments of crisis, the Austrians had managed to impose their views by threatening war against Serbia and Montenegro. Secondly, the Germans showed increasing signs of committing themselves to an ambitious policy in the near east both by supporting Austria-Hungary in the Balkans and by turning Turkey into a satellite (**108, 171**). One of the most consistent elements in the policy of Wilhelm II had been the encouragement of German interests in the near east, and by 1914 Germany was the most important foreign component in the Turkish economy (**75**). More worrying still in Russian eyes was the appointment of a German general, Liman von Sanders, to command the Turkish garrison at Constantinople. If this permitted Germany to control the Straits in a moment of crisis it could place Russia in a very difficult position, as more than one-third of her trade passed through them (**182**). By 1914 it had become an axiom of Russia's policy that, although there was no compelling need for her to take Constantinople for herself, she would fight rather than allow a foreign power to do so [**doc. 10**].

Russia's fears of German ambitions in the near east were not unjustified (**166**). In the autumn of 1913 Wilhelm II had assured both the chief of the general staff and the foreign minister of Austria-Hungary that the time for decisive military action in the Balkans was drawing near and that Germany could be relied upon for support. In February 1914 Russian military intelligence intercepted two German memoranda that expressed determination to capture Constantinople should the Ottoman empire collapse, and to prepare German public opinion for the coming war with Russia and France. These revelations convinced the Russians that a combined Austro-German effort would soon be made to establish predominance in the Balkans and at the Straits. They replied to this threat by consolidating their relationship with France and Britain and by relying upon Serbia – with her army of 200,000 men and 200,000 reservists – to act as the bastion against further Austrian expansion (**249**).

Ironically, considering these Russian fears, the Austrians and the Germans had reason to believe that their situation was deteriorating. The Schlieffen plan of 1905, and Moltke's revision of it in 1911, was dependent upon the ability of Austro-German forces to keep Russia at bay while the Germans knocked out the French in the west; the German strategists believed that this was the only method by which they could hope to win a two-front war. The role that had been assigned to Austria-Hungary was an offensive one: she was to launch an attack through Galicia, which would force a significant part of the Russian army to stand on the defensive (**133**). But this scheme was laid before the Balkan wars and the consequent growth in the size and power of Serbia, which now meant that Austria-Hungary would have to commit half her forces to the south if a crisis began there (**73**). At the same time, Russian military strength appeared to be growing rapidly: a 'Great Military Programme' had been adopted in November 1913 that provided for a 40 per cent increase in the size of the standing army over the next four years, and this was to be supplemented with the rapidly expanding railway network – made possible by French loans and by the industrial revolution going on in the Ukraine (**250**).

Wilhelm II's apparently wild encouragement to the Austrians to settle the Serbian question once and for all was not as irrational as it seems. If the danger in the south were removed Austria-Hungary could again concentrate her forces against Russia. When the Austrian successor to the throne was assassinated on 28 June in Sarajevo by a Serb nationalist therefore, a situation seemed to have presented itself that was tailor-made to suit German requirements: Austria-Hungary could 'settle' the Serbs, who were unlikely to receive much support, given the facts of the assassination; while France and Britain had never shown much inclination to support Russia's Balkan policy in the past [**doc. 12**] (**67**).

When, on 4 July, the emperor Francis-Joseph wrote to Wilhelm II that he proposed to 'eliminate Serbia as a power factor in the Balkans' he received a sympathetic response. After consulting his chancellor, Bethmann Hollweg, the kaiser urged Austria-Hungary to make war on Serbia, issuing what is referred to as the 'blank cheque' in assuring the Austrians of support even if it meant war with Russia [**doc. 11**] (**151, 156**). But the kaiser did not believe that Russia would intervene, for this would require the tsar to come out in support of assassins – a most unlikely stance. The kaiser therefore left Germany on a cruise and no preparations for war were made. The Germans believed that they had a great diplomatic victory in their grasp (**174, 195**).

Speed was essential to such a victory. Austria-Hungary would have to act quickly and decisively to present a *fait accompli* while the memory of the assassination was still vivid. But Austrian counsels were divided: foreign minister Berchtold proposed to launch a surprise attack, while the Hungarian prime minister, Count Tisza, insisted that some diplomatic preparation was necessary if Austria-Hungary was not to be branded as an aggressor (**185**). Tisza proposed to issue a list of stiff, but not impossible, demands to Serbia, which, if accepted, would be a great diplomatic triumph (**196**). The rest of the ministers agreed on 7 July to the idea of demands and that there should be no mobilisation until these were rejected and an ultimatum issued; on the other hand they accepted that the demands should be so extreme as to guarantee rejection. This decision slowed down the process so much that it practically negated the original German plan. The note containing the demands and the ultimatum was not presented until 23 July – almost three weeks after the blank cheque had been issued [**doc. 15**] (**186**).

When the Russian foreign minister, Sazonov, received a copy of the demands on 24 July he immediately concluded that the Austrians knew they would be unacceptable and must be designed as a prelude to war with Serbia. He also believed that the Austrians would not have gone this far had they not been certain of German support. At a council of ministers that day, Sazonov maintained that if Serbia were abandoned to Austria-Hungary, Russia's position in the Balkans would 'collapse utterly'; and, as the crisis was being used by the Germans to increase their power in central Europe and the near east, Russia would henceforth be considered a decadent state and slip into the ranks of the second-rate if she failed to take a strong stand (**215**). The defence ministers, while they could not guarantee military superiority over the central powers, counselled that there was no military reason why Russia should not display firmness in diplomatic negotiations. That evening Serbia was assured of Russia's continuing support.

It is questionable whether Russia would have responded so decisively had she not been assured of French support. Poincaré, however, had insisted upon the closest possible connection with Russia as the most vital ingredient of his foreign policy. He had decided, in contrast with the Bosnian crisis of 1908, that France could not jeopardise that alliance with Russia by once again failing to support her in the Balkans; if Russia were forced to yield in the Balkans it would encourage the pro-German group to insist upon a reconciliation with Germany. If Russia were reconciled to Germany, if the French alliance with Russia were dissolved, the balance of power in Europe would be destroyed and France would no longer be capable of acting as an independent great power (**221, 227**).

On the other hand, as the Russians hoped to avoid a crisis with Germany and to keep the Serbian affair a strictly Austro-Russian matter, the support of France may not have been decisive; certainly the ambiguous and uncertain attitude of Britain did nothing to restrain Russia. The Russians, on 24–25 July, undertook military measures preliminary to mobilisation; but they attempted to localise the crisis by preparing to mobilise only in the military districts of Odessa, Kiev, Kazan and Moscow in order to show their determination to intervene if Austria-Hungary attacked Serbia, while avoiding any direct challenge to Germany.

Any lingering doubts there may have been in Russia concerning Austria's intentions were dissipated by the Austrian rejection of the Serbian reply to their demands. The Serbs had, in the opinion of the Russians, French and British, gone much further in the attempt to accommodate Austria-Hungary than they had believed possible (**189**). The Austrians, on 28 July, the day after the reply was received, declared war on Serbia; the next day Belgrade was shelled. On 30 July the Russian government was convinced by the military authorities that a partial mobilisation was impossible; it therefore ordered a general mobilisation [**doc. 16**] (**223**).

The German military authorities had by this time come round to the view that, as war seemed likely, and as Austria-Hungary could not be abandoned if she were to fight Russia, this moment was more propitious than any in the foreseeable future. The French, they argued, were not prepared for a fight, while the Russians would only continue to grow stronger with each passing year. Moltke was convinced that, even if Britain did enter the war, France would be overrun in spite of the 150,000 men of the British expeditionary force. The Russian mobilisation played directly into the hands of the militarists: they could now argue that if Germany failed to respond immediately her strategic plans would be negated, and that the German people as a whole would support the war effort because Russia had taken the initiative. On the morning of 31 July, therefore, Germany mobilised and insisted that Russia cease all military measures aimed at Germany and Austria-Hungary within twelve hours. No reply came. Germany declared war on Russia at 6 p.m. on 1 August (**157**).

The most fateful step had been taken. Once Germany declared war on Russia, France had little choice but to join in. Not to have done so would have signalled her end as a great power. This was made abundantly clear on 1 August when the Germans asked what the French attitude would be in the event of a Russo-German war – while telling the French that, should they choose to remain neutral, they would have to surrender the fortresses on their eastern frontier. In other words, Germany must be clearly victorious, with or without fighting. France replied by announcing mobilisation. Two days later Germany declared war on France; on 4 August she invaded Belgium.

An awful sense of pre-ordination surrounds the events of the first days of August. Certainly each step down the road to war from the Austrian ultimatum onwards appears logical and irreversible. But this could not be foreseen prior to the events. Italy, for example, was not drawn into the abyss as a result of her prior commitments. On 3 August she declared her neutrality. Her partners in the Triple Alliance had practically ignored her during the crisis, mainly because they distrusted her, but also because they had a low opinion of her abilities as a great power. They offered her nothing in exchange for honouring her commitments. Thus, if Italy had chosen to side with Germany and Austria-Hungary in spite of these snubs, she would have confirmed her role as a weak and subordinate member of the alliance, and could expect to be treated as such in the future. The Italians, calmly and rationally, chose to remain on the sidelines and wait upon events.

Although the British reached a different conclusion, they too refused to be drawn into the war as if their participation had been predetermined. As the crisis unfolded, Grey made it clear to Russia and France that Britain was entirely free from commitments (**264**). In spite of repeated efforts to include Britain in a demonstration of entente solidarity, Grey feared that such a demonstration would alarm the Germans and deepen the crisis; he counselled moderation and direct negotiations between Russia and Austria-Hungary. Even when the Austrians presented their ultimatum – the seriousness of which Grey fully recognised – and then spurned the Serbian reply, Grey refused to take any dramatic steps. His advisers at the foreign office were distressed: from the time of the ultimatum they were convinced that the crisis was being used by Germany to achieve her ambition of political domination in Europe. On the other hand, he kept those members of the cabinet who were known to be opposed to any British armed intervention in the dark concerning the details of the crisis and the expectations of support in France and Russia (**269**).

Grey was determined to avoid a conflict if at all possible, but he also believed that Britain would have to assist France if she went to war with Germany. In the last days of July he began to prepare the cabinet for the worst. Germany, he warned, did not seem interested in mediation and appeared to be doing nothing to restrain Austria-Hungary. On 29 July the majority of the cabinet refused to agree to his proposal that they should promise to support France; they even refused to promise to uphold the neutrality of Belgium that had been guaranteed by treaty in 1839 – if Belgian neutrality were violated, the British decision would be 'one of policy rather than legal obligation'. On 1 August Grey was forced to tell the French ambassador that a British expeditionary force might not be sent to France, even if Britain were to enter the war. On the next day the cabinet, following a plea from France, did agree to warn the Germans that Britain would not tolerate any naval action by her in the Channel or on the French coast; but the Germans readily assented to this provision. What was significant about the decision of 2 August was that a large majority of the cabinet finally agreed that British policy had to be one of support for the entente, despite their continuing confusion over what form this support ought to take. One minister, John Burns, resigned; the others who opposed intervention realised that if they forced the issue, the government would fall, probably to be replaced by a coalition that would intervene anyway (**279, 281**).

The violation of Belgian neutrality by Germany on 4 August provided a convenient justification for those in the cabinet who had already reluctantly decided that intervention was inevitable. They could now claim to have supported war for reasons of morality and law. Britain's entry into the war had little to do with Belgium – if Germany had not invaded there might have been a few more resignations, but nothing more than this. Britain would have intervened in any case, believing that this was essential to preserve the balance of power and prevent the German domination of Europe [**doc. 14**]. On 6 August it was agreed to send the expeditionary force to France. Within a week the five great powers were at war.

Part Four: Assessment

The most persistent assumption underlying the decisions of July 1914 was the illusion that the war would be short. The thinking behind this was relatively simple: modern methods of transportation and communication created unprecedented opportunities for speed and mobility in attack. This was the lesson of the Franco-Prussian war of 1870. The Prussian use of railways had been decisive; the French, after all, had had as many men under arms and were, in every measurable category, as powerful as the Germans. The difference, it was believed, was to be found in the Prussian ability to harness the new possibilities for warfare to be found in industrial society. The experience of the Russo-Japanese war and the Balkan wars was discounted accordingly; they were not fought by peoples or in regions to which the new technology applied. All the war plans of the great powers before 1914 hinged upon railway timetables and the rapid deployment of men in the field.

The belief in speed was crucial. The most famous stratagem, the Schlieffen plan, called for a lightning attack on France's western flank – but this was not exceptional; in France, Joffre proposed a quick strike through Alsace in his Plan 17; in Russia, Plan B called for Russia to seize the offensive and attack through Poland; in Austria-Hungary, the alliance with Germany provided for an attack on Russia to be launched from Galicia; in Great Britain, the planning for the British Expeditionary Force assumed that it must land in France within days of war being declared in order for it to be effective. These plans showed the extent to which strategists committed themselves to the view that standing on the defensive would lead to ruin (**183, 254, 280**). The Germans believed that they had to defeat France quickly to enable them to concentrate their full attention on Russia – and that an Austrian offensive against Russia would be vital in allowing them time to defeat France; the Russians believed that only an overwhelming attack in the east could prevent the Germans from overrunning France (**84, 242**).

Although these strategic calculations turned out to be ill-founded they were essential to the decisions made in July. Once the steps towards mobilisation began, everyone assumed that it would be fatal to stand idle while others seized the initiative. Especially crucial in this respect were the Russian mobilisation and the German response. When Russia attempted to mobilise against Austria-Hungary alone she discovered that this was practically impossible as she had made no plans for such a contingency; moreover it would make a general mobilisation extremely difficult should it prove impossible to localise the war in the Balkans (**100**). If the Germans had permitted the Russian mobilisation to be carried through without responding in kind, it would have jeopardised what was regarded as their only feasible plan for fighting a major war. By 28–30 July the generals had taken over from the politicians and the nature of their plans made war among the great powers a virtual certainty (**94, 136**).

It is also true that Germany had really decided to force a war before Russia mobilised. Although the war plans are important in understanding why the crisis unfolded in the way that it did, they provide only a partial answer to the question, 'why did the war begin?' Ultimately, the Germans' decision to force a war with Russia was not determined so much by railway timetables as by their belief that they could not permit Austria-Hungary to be defeated and that, if a war for the future of the Balkans and the near east had to be fought some time, the best time was now (**99**). It is tempting, given this Austro-German connection on the one hand, and the Franco-Russian on the other, to regard the alliance 'system' as the real cause of the war.

The system, however, worked far from systematically in July 1914. First, Italy refused to come to the assistance of her allies. Germany and Austria-Hungary alike distrusted her and kept her in the dark when critical decisions were being made (**137, 212**). The Triple Alliance turned out not to be a Triplice after all. Nor did the 'Triple Entente' operate as an alliance. No one, not the Russians, not the French, not the Central Powers, knew what Britain's response to the crisis would be. The Russian decision to mobilise was taken in spite of the absence of any guarantee of support from the British; the German decision to force a war with Russia was taken when the attitude of the British was still uncertain. The British case shows that not all of the great powers were committed to act; the Italian case shows that even when commitments existed these could be ignored if it seemed to be in someone's interest to ignore them. It was not the alliance 'system' that drew the great powers into war in 1914, but the belief that it was more dangerous to stay out of a war than enter into one (**112, 213**).

Each of the great powers decided in 1914 that they had vital interests at stake – interests for which it was worth risking defeat, dismemberment, impoverishment and social revolution. Had they anticipated the extent of the carnage, the duration of the war, the political and social chaos that it caused, they might have made different decisions. But it is doubtful. By and large the men who made the decisions, drawn mainly from the traditional ruling classes of Europe, believed it better to die honourably than to survive in disgrace – and this applied to their states as well as to themselves. This was especially true of the eastern powers, Austria-Hungary, Russia and Germany, who felt they were already teetering on the brink of a disaster, and that war (which they hoped and assumed would be successful) was the only alternative to a humiliating diplomatic defeat (**113, 126, 263, 270**).

What distinguished the July crisis from those of the previous decade? It was not the existence of war plans or a system of alliances, but the fact that in these earlier crises one or more of the leading participants took the view that the interests at stake did not justify the risk of war. Nor would it have been easy to persuade people to take up arms on behalf of some of the issues involved in these crises: few Germans were convinced that the economic stake in Morocco was worth a war with France; few Russians could have been persuaded that the change from an Austrian occupation of Bosnia and Herzegovina to a protectorate was worth fighting to stop. The crisis of July 1914 was exceptional in that the issues at stake made it possible for each of the great powers to mobilise the public support without which war would have been impossible.

The first fateful step towards war was taken by Austria-Hungary when her government decided that the moment had come to 'solve' the problem of Slav nationalism when the heir to the throne was assassinated at Sarajevo. Such an opportunity was not likely to come again. Although the actual extent of complicity on the part of Serbian officials was not known at the time, all of the great powers expected Austria-Hungary to take some action against Serbia, and they accepted this as justified; each of the 'entente' powers urged Serbia to be as accommodating as possible when she replied to the Austrian ultimatum – and they would have accepted the considerable limitations on her independence that her reply involved. Moreover, the assassination provided more than a pretext: it offered a possibility of mobilising public sentiment throughout the Dual Monarchy in favour of vigorous action; any future attempt to 'solve' the Slav problem was unlikely to occur in such favourable circumstances. Finally, Germany's strong encouragement to act decisively and crush the Serbian threat once and for all was decisive: her support had been essential in the Bosnian crisis of 1909, and without it Austria-Hungary would not have dared to risk war with Russia. Thus, it may be legitimately argued that a substantial underlying cause of the war was nationalism in general, and in particular the demand for unified, independent states in the Balkans and the threat this posed to the antiquated structure of multi-national Austria-Hungary (**190**).

But there would not have been a war if Russia had declined to mobilise in support of Serbia. The Russian decision to do so was made simultaneously on several levels. First, the strategic calculation was that Russia could not permit the transformation of Serbia into a satellite of Austria-Hungary because this would lead to an Austrian domination of the Balkans which, when combined with Germany's expanding role in Turkey, might allow the Central Powers to dominate most of the near east. If Austria-Hungary and Germany dominated the Balkans and the Straits it would make the defence of Russia extremely difficult and endanger vital Russian trade. Secondly, support for the Slavic peoples was the one programme that tied together almost all elements of influential Russian society. Whereas the war against Japan had been popular with only a narrow element, and whereas a war against Britain in central Asia would have stirred up little emotional support, almost all sectors of the Russian political community believed that Russia was destined to perform a great cultural and religious task in south-eastern Europe. In fact, the Russian government would have been severely shaken by opposition had it failed to respond forcefully to Austria-Hungary's ultimatum. Thirdly, in contrast with 1909, the French had assured the Russians of support in the Balkans – and it was highly unlikely that, if the Russians now backed down and allowed the Central Powers to prevail, such support would again be available in the future. Thus, it may be argued that the Russian version of Slav nationalism was an underlying cause of the war, because for the government to have abandoned its historical mission would have shaken the cultural foundations of the tsarist state.

The July crisis was, in essence, an Austro-Russian one; the transformation of that crisis into a world war was the responsibility of Germany (**130, 131**). The German government decided immediately following the assassination that the perfect opportunity had arisen by which Austria-Hungary could dissipate much of the internal unrest that plagued her while simultaneously reducing the Balkans to an order that suited Austro-German interests. This was not a decision calculated to precipitate a war but rather one which looked forward to a diplomatic triumph even more dramatic than that of 1909. The triumph would strengthen Austria-Hungary while attaching her to Germany even more closely in the future. The fateful moment came when Russia undertook a partial mobilisation, which made it clear that she would not back down this time. Faced with this determined Russian response, Germany had either to go backward, restrain her ally and admit to diplomatic defeat, or go forward and threaten Russia with war. She chose to go forward (**135, 142, 144, 150**).

The thinking behind Germany's decision was both military and political. Her military leaders advised that her position relative to Russia would deteriorate over the next few years: the Russian army would be expanded at a rate that Germany could not hope to match; the Russian economy appeared to have passed through the first stages of an industrial revolution; plans for railway construction, if they were realised, would allow the Russians to maximise the advantage they enjoyed in their numbers of fighting men (**159**). Politically, German leaders concluded that they had been 'encircled' by Russia, France and Great Britain, and that successive diplomatic crises had demonstrated that it was impossible to break out of this combination by peaceful means (**117, 181**). The German landowners and bourgeoisie were also generally inclined to believe that a great victorious war would enable them to triumph over those elements in German society, particularly the socialists of the industrial cities, opposed to the rule of the traditional élite. The most significant of the underlying causes of the war was the dynamic growth of German power in the decades that preceded it, and the fact that the management of that power resided with an élite who were accustomed to believe that war was an attractive policy that usually brought them social, political and economic rewards (**85**).

The German, Russian and Austrian decisions were the momentous ones. Given Moltke's revision of the Schlieffen plan, France was bound to be attacked, no matter what she did. Her role was significant nevertheless. Had Russia not been repeatedly assured by Poincaré, since he came into power in 1912, of French assist-

ance in any future Balkan crisis, she might have been more reluctant to support Serbia to the point of war with Austria-Hungary.
Furthermore, without the Russian alliance, which almost all
France's statesmen regarded as indispensable to her foreign
policy, it is possible that the Schlieffen plan would not have been
formulated. But the French believed that without the Russian
alliance there would be no balance of power and France would
inevitably succumb to the domination of Germany. The French
decision, therefore, was not made on the basis of *revanche* for the
'lost provinces' of Alsace and Lorraine. National pride was significant in encouraging French politicians to fight for France's
survival as an independent great power (**234, 244**).

Of the five great powers who went to war in August 1914,
Britain played the least significant part. Her support, or lack of it,
neither encouraged nor restrained Russia and France. While some
have argued that war might have been averted if she had made it
evident early in the crisis that she would join Russia and France
in the fighting, this seems doubtful. The German military – as well
as the French – took little account of Britain's ability to contribute
substantially to the fighting; their plans hinged upon the quick
knock-out blow of France, and they assumed that this would have
been achieved before Britain could do much about it. Had they
anticipated a four-year-long war of attrition they would perhaps
have rated Britain more highly. It might just as easily be argued
that if Britain had taken a strong and committed line from the start
she would simply have confirmed the argument of those Germans
who believed that she was behind the policy of encirclement, and
that an armed conflict was the only way whereby Germany could
break up the coalition that had been organised to contain her.

The British had done their best in the decade before 1914 to
show France that they would stand by her if she were threatened
by Germany, but they consistently refused to commit themselves
in advance of events (**117**). This was not due to Liberal fuzzy-
mindedness or adherence to tradition, but to a realistic appraisal
of the situation on the continent. The British rated themselves
more highly than the Germans did; consequently, they believed
that if the French and/or the Russians were guaranteed British
support in a war they would be more intransigent in times of crisis
and might even provoke a war. The British were nevertheless
drawn reluctantly into the war because they believed that a victorious Germany would inevitably dominate the continent. The
British empire was in no immediate danger; Britain did not go to

war in order to crush the German fleet, but to save France. The naval race had helped to embitter the British public against Germany, to turn their animosity away from the traditional enemies, France and Russia; and the German invasion of Belgium was instrumental in confirming the British in the righteousness of their cause. But the men making the decisions would have led Britain into war regardless of the invasion of Belgium (**262, 273**).

The First World War was not inevitable. Although it is essential to understand the underlying factors that formed the background to the July crisis, it is equally essential to see how the immediate circumstances of the crisis fit into this background in a particular, and perhaps unique, way (**123**). Europe was not a powder-keg waiting to explode; one crisis did not lead necessarily to another in an escalating series of confrontations that made war more and more difficult to avoid. Europe had successfully weathered a number of storms in the recent past; the alliances were not rigidly fixed; the war plans were always being revised and need not necessarily have come into play. It is difficult to imagine a crisis in the far east, in north Africa or the Mediterranean that would have unleashed the series of events that arose from the assassination in Sarajevo (**118**). The First World War was, in the final analysis, fought for the future of the near east; whoever won this struggle would, it was believed, be in a position to dominate all of Europe. Germany and her ally made the bid for control; Russia and her allies resolved to stop them (**87, 144, 166**).

Part Five: Documents

document 1
The Dual Alliance

This alliance between Germany and Austria was signed on 7 October 1879, and consisted of four articles. Articles III and IV provided for a five-year renewable term for the treaty and for it to be kept secret – but the tsar was to be informed that an attack on either of the signatories would be regarded as an attack on both.

ART. I. Should, contrary to their hope, and against the loyal desire of the two High Contracting Parties, one of the two Empires be attacked by Russia, the High Contracting Parties are bound to come to the assistance one of the other with the whole war strength of their Empires, and accordingly only to conclude peace together and upon mutual agreement.

ART. II. Should one of the High Contracting Parties be attacked by another Power, the other High Contracting Party binds itself hereby, not only not to support the aggressor against its high Ally, but to observe at least a benevolent neutral attitude towards its fellow Contracting Party.

Should, however, the attacking party in such a case be supported by Russia, either by an active co-operation or by military measures which constitute a menace to the Party attacked, then the obligation stipulated in Article I of this Treaty, for reciprocal assistance with the whole fighting force, becomes equally operative, and the conduct of the war by the two High Contracting Parties shall in this case also be in common until the conclusion of a common peace.

Reprinted in *Key Treaties for the Great Powers 1814–1914*, Vol 2: *1871–1914*, ed. Michael Hurst, David and Charles, 1974, p. 590

document 2

The Triple Alliance

This treaty between Austria-Hungary, Germany and Italy was signed on 20 May 1882. Further articles provided for a term of five years and for it to remain secret.

ART. I. The High Contracting Parties mutually promise peace and friendship, and will enter into no alliance or engagement directed against any one of their States.

They engage to proceed to an exchange of ideas on political and economic questions of a general nature which may arise, and they further promise one another mutual support within the limits of their own interests.

ART. II. In case Italy, without direct provocation on her part, should be attacked by France for any reason whatsoever, the two other Contracting Parties shall be bound to lend help and assistance with all their forces to the Party attacked.

This same obligation shall devolve upon Italy in case of any aggression without direct provocation by France against Germany.

ART III. If one, or two, of the High Contracting Parties, without direct provocation on their part, should chance to be attacked and to be engaged in a war with two or more Great Powers nonsignatory to the present Treaty, the *casus foederis* will arise simultaneously for all the High Contracting Parties.

ART. IV. In case a Great Power nonsignatory to the present Treaty should threaten the security of the states of one of the High contracting Parties, and the threatened Party should find itself forced on that account to make war against it, the two others bind themselves to observe towards their Ally a benevolent neutrality. Each of them reserves to itself, in this case, the right to take part in the war, if it should see fit, to make common cause with its Ally.

ART. V. If the peace of any of the High Contracting Parties should chance to be threatened under the circumstances foreseen by the preceding Articles, the High Contracting Parties shall take counsel together in ample time as to the military measures to be taken with a view to eventual co-operation.

They engage henceforward, in all cases of common participation in a war, to conclude neither armistice, nor peace, nor treaty, except by common agreement among themselves.

Key Treaties, pp. 611–2

document 3
Bismarck's Eastern Policy

After his resignation in 1890, Bismarck was anxious to clarify the difference between his conservative policy in the East, and the apparently adventurous one of Wilhelm II.

... in the future not only military equipment but also a correct political eye will be required to guide the German ship of state through the currents of coalitions to which we are exposed in consequence of our geographical position and our previous history. We shall not avoid the dangers which lie in the bosom of the future by amiability and commercial *pourboires* to friendly Powers. We should only increase the greed of our former friends and teach them to reckon on our anxieties and necessities ... Our reputation and our security will develop all the more permanently, the more, in all conflicts which do not immediately touch us, we hold ourselves in reserve and do not show ourselves sensitive to every attempt to stir up and utilise our *vanity* ... Germany would be guilty of a great folly if in Eastern struggles which did not affect her interests she were to take a side sooner than the other Powers who were more directly concerned ... in future Eastern negotiations Germany, by holding back, will be able to turn to its advantage the fact that it is the Power which has least interest in Oriental questions ...

If Germany has the advantage that her policy is free from direct interests in the East, on the other side is the disadvantage of the central and exposed position of the German Empire, with its extended frontier which has to be defended on every side, and the ease with which anti-German coalitions are made. At the same time Germany is perhaps the single Great Power in Europe which is not tempted by any objects which can only be attained by a successful war. It is our interest to maintain peace, while without exception our continental neighbours have wishes, either secret or officially avowed, which cannot be fulfilled except by war ... we must do our best to prevent war or limit it.

Otto von Bismarck, *Bismarck: The Memoirs*, Vol. 2, Howard Fertig, 1966, pp. 290–2

document 4

The Reinsurance Treaty

This treaty was signed between Germany and Russia on 18 June 1887 and was to remain in force for three years.

ART. I. In case one of the High Contracting Parties should find itself at war with a third great Power, the other would maintain a benevolent neutrality towards it, and would devote its efforts to the localization of the conflict. This provision would not apply to a war against Austria or France in case this war should result from an attack directed against one of these two latter Powers by one of the High Contracting Parties.

ART. II. Germany recognizes the rights historically acquired by Russia in the Balkan Peninsula, and particularly the legitimacy of her preponderant and decisive influence in Bulgaria and in Eastern Rumelia. The two Courts engage to admit no modification of the territorial status quo of the said peninsula without a previous agreement between them, and to oppose, as occasion arises, every attempt to disturb this status quo or to modify it without their consent.

ART. III. The two Courts recognize the European and mutually obligatory character of the principle of the closing of the Straits of the Bosphorus and of the Dardanelles, founded on international law, confirmed by treaties, and summed up in the declaration of the second Plenipotentiary of Russia at the session of July 12 of the Congress of Berlin (Protocol 19).

They will take care in common that Turkey shall make no exception to this rule in favour of the interests of any Government whatsoever, by lending to warlike operations of a belligerent power the portion of its Empire constituted by the Straits. In case of infringement, or to prevent it if such infringement should be in prospect, the two Courts will inform Turkey that they would regard her, in that event, as putting herself in a state of war towards the injured Party, and as depriving herself thenceforth of the benefits of the security assured to her territorial status quo by the Treaty of Berlin.

Key Treaties, p. 646

document 5
The 'Willy-Nicky' Correspondence

Wilhelm II hoped, by means of a friendly personal correspondence with Nicholas II (conducted in English), to deflect Russia's ambitions from Europe to Asia, and to arouse the tsar's fears of too close a relationship with revolutionary France.

26 April 1895

. . . I shall certainly do all in my power to keep Europe quiet, and also guard the rear of Russia so that nobody shall hamper your action towards the Far East!

For that is clearly the great task of the future for Russia to cultivate the Asian Continent and to defend Europe from the inroads of the Great Yellow race. In this you will always find me on your side, ready to help you as best I can . . .

26 September 1895

. . . The proposed new Corps would increase the already over-whelming French forces to 5 Corps, and constitutes a threat as well as a serious danger to my country . . . [it] has made people uneasy here and given affairs an ugly look, as if Russia would like France to be offensive against Germany with the hopes of help from the first named . . . *I* perfectly know that *you* personally do not dream of attacking us, but still you cannot be astonished that the Euro-pean Powers get alarmed seeing how the presence of your officers and high officials in *official way* in France fans the inflamable [sic] Frenchman into a white heated passion and strengthens the cause of Chauvinism and Revanche! . . . if France goes on openly or secretly encouraged like this to violate all rules of international courtesy and Peace in peace times, one fine day my dearest Nicky you will find yourself *nolens volens* suddenly embroiled in the most horrible of wars Europe ever saw! . . .

25 October 1895

. . . it is not a *fact* of the *Rapport* or friendship between Russia and France that makes one uneasy . . . but the danger which is brought to our Principle of Monarchism through the lifting up [of] the Republic on a pedestal by the form under which the friendship is shown. The constant appearance of Princes, Grand-dukes, statesmen, Generals in 'full fig' at reviews, burials, dinners, races, with the head of the Republic or in his entourage makes Republicains [sic] . . . believe that they are quite honest excellent people with whom Princes can consort and feel at home! . . . Don't forget that Jaurès . . . sits on the throne of the King and Queen of France 'by the Grace of God' whose heads Frenchmen Republicans cut off! The Blood of their Majesties is still on that country! Look at it, has it since then ever been happy or quiet again? Has it not staggered from bloodshed to bloodshed? And in its great moments did it not go from war to war? Till it soused all Europe and Russia in streams of blood? Till at last it had the Commune over again? Nicky take my word on it the curse of God has stricken that people forever!

If unfortunately, as a result of a mature examination of the situation, Germany and Italy should both recognize that the maintenance of the status quo has become impossible, Germany engages, after a formal and previous agreement, to support Italy in any action in the form of occupation or other taking of guaranty which the latter should undertake in these same regions with a view to an interest of equilibrium and of legitimate compensation.

It is understoood that in such an eventuality the two Powers would seek to place themselves likewise in agreement with England.

Kaiser Wilhelm II, (**30**), pp. 10–11, 20–1, 23–5

document 6

The Franco-Russian Alliance

The alliance between France and Russia was founded upon an exchange of letters between their foreign ministers in August 1891; the alliance was not formally ratified until the following year.

Letter of M. de Giers, Minister of Foreign Affairs of Russia, to M. de Mohrenheim, Ambassador of Russia at Paris. Petersburg, August 9/21, 1891.

The situation created in Europe by the open renewal of the Triple Alliance and the more or less probable adhesion of Great Britain to the political aims which that alliance pursues, has, during the recent sojourn here of M. de Laboulaye, prompted an exchange of ideas between the former Ambassador of France and myself, tending to define the attitude which, as things now stand and in the presence of certain eventualities, might best suit our respective Governments, which, having kept out of any league, are none the less sincerely desirous of surrounding the maintenance of peace with the most efficacious guarantees.

It is thus that we have been led to formulate the two points below:
1. In order to define and consecrate the cordial understanding which unites them, and desirous of contributing in common agreement to the maintenance of the peace which forms the object of their sincerest aspirations, the two Governments declare that they will take counsel together upon every question of a nature to jeopardize the general peace;
2. In case that peace should be actually in danger, and especially if one of the two parties should be threatened with an aggression, the two parties undertake to reach an understanding on the measures whose immediate and simultaneous adoption would be imposed upon the two Governments by the realization of this eventuality . . .

Key Treaties, p. 663

document 7
Franco-Russian Military Convention

The military co-operation provided for in document 9 was outlined in this 1892 draft agreement, which was approved in December 1893.

France and Russia, being animated by an equal desire to preserve peace, and having no other object than to meet the necessities of a defensive war, provoked by an attack of the forces of the Triple Alliance against the one or the other of them, have agreed upon the following provisions:
1. If France is attacked by Germany, or by Italy supported by Germany, Russia shall employ all her available forces to attack Germany.

If Russia is attacked by Germany, or by Austria supported by Germany, France shall employ all her available forces to fight Germany.

2. In case the forces of the Triple Alliance, or of one of the Powers composing it, should mobilize, France and Russia, at the first news of the event and without the necessity of any previous concert, shall mobilize immediately and simultaneously the whole of their forces and shall move them as close as possible to their frontiers.

3. The available forces to be employed against Germany shall be, on the part of France, 1,300,000 men, on the part of Russia, 700,000 or 800,000 men.

These forces shall engage to the full, with all speed, in order that Germany may have to fight at the same time on the East and on the West.

4. The General Staffs of the Armies of the two countries shall co-operate with each other at all times in the preparation and facilitation of the execution of the measures above foreseen.

They shall communicate to each other, while there is still peace, all information relative to the armies of the Triple Alliance which is or shall be within their knowledge.

Ways and means of corresponding in times of war shall be studied and arranged in advance.

5. France and Russia shall not conclude peace separately.

6. The present Convention shall have the same duration as the Triple Alliance.

7. All the clauses above enumerated shall be kept rigorously secret.

Key Treaties, pp. 668–9

document 8

Germany and 'World Policy'

The German Chancellor, Prince von Bülow, explained in a speech to the Reichstag on 11 December 1899 why the deputies must support a large army and navy.

. . recent decades have brought to Germany great good fortune and power and prosperity. Good fortune and growing prosperity in one quarter are not always greeted in others with pure satisfaction; they may awaken envy. Envy plays a great part in the life of individuals and in the life of nations. There is a great deal of envy of us in the world, political envy and economic envy . . . [the] times of political impotence and economic and political insignificance must not return. We do not intend again to be . . . the bondmen of humanity. The one condition, however, on which alone we shall maintain our position is that we realize that without power, without a strong army and a strong navy, there can be no welfare for us. The means of fighting the battle for existence in this world without strong armaments on land and water, for a nation soon to count sixty millions, living in the centre of Europe and at the same time stretching out its economic feelers in all directions, have not yet been found. In the coming century the German nation will be either the hammer or the anvil.

Prince von Bülow, (**16**), p. 353

The Anglo-Japanese Alliance

document 9

This agreement was made on 30 January 1902; further articles provided for consultation in case the interests of either signatory were jeopardised, and for a renewable term of five years.

ART. I. The High Contracting Parties, having mutually recognised the independence of China and Korea, declare themselves to be entirely uninfluenced by any aggressive tendencies in either country. Having in view, however, their special interests of which those of Great Britain relate principally to China, while Japan, in addition to the interests which she possesses in China, is interested in a peculiar degree politically as well as commercially and industrially in Korea, the High Contracting Parties recognise that it will be admissible for either of them to take such measures as may be indispensable in order to safeguard those interests if threatened either by the aggressive action of any other Power, or by disturbances arising in China or Korea, and necessitating the intervention of either of the High Contracting Parties for the protection of the lives and property of its subjects.

ART. II. If either Great Britain or Japan, in the defence of their respective interests as above described, should become involved in war with another Power, the other High Contracting Party will maintain a strict neutrality, and use its efforts to prevent other Powers from joining in hostilities against its ally.

ART. III. If, in the above event, any other Power or Powers should join in hostilities against that ally, the other High Contracting

Party will come to its assistance, and will conduct the war in common, and make peace in mutual agreement with it.

Key Treaties, pp. 726–7

document 10
Russia's Balkan Policy

Although the memoirs and autobiographies of the leading participants in the events of 1914 are invariably self-serving, they are still of interest to the student. Here the Russian Foreign Minister, Serge Sazonov, explains both the idealist and the practical components of Russian policy.

. . . Russia's historical mission – the emancipation of the Christian peoples of the Balkan peninsula from the Turkish yoke – was almost fulfilled by the beginning of the twentieth century; its completion could be left to the efforts of the liberated peoples themselves . . . Although these younger countries no longer needed the guardianship of Russia, they were not yet strong enough to dispense with her help in the event of any attempt upon their national existence by warlike Teutonism. Serbia in particular was exposed to this danger, having become the object of the decorously concealed covetousness of Austrian diplomacy . . . [Russia's] sole and unchanging object was to see that those Balkan peoples who had been freed by her age-long efforts and sacrifices should not fall under the influence of Powers hostile to her, or become the obedient tools of their political intrigues. The ultimate aim of Russian policy was to obtain free access to the Mediterranean, and to be in a position to defend her Black Sea coasts against the constant threat of the irruption of hostile naval forces through the Bosphorus . . .

Russia proclaimed and defended the principle of the independence of the Balkan States as fundamentally just, in view of their inalienable right to an independent political existence. In our eyes this principle, in addition to its moral significance, had also a practical value; for not only was it not detrimental to any of Russia's vital interests, but it indirectly furthered their maintenance. 'The Balkan Peninsula for the Balkan peoples' was the formula which comprised the aspirations and aims of Russian policy; it precluded the possibility of the political predominance, and still more of the sovereignty in the Balkans, of a foreign Power hostile to Balkan Slavdom and to Russia.

S. Sazonov, (**54**), pp. 49–51

The Kaiser's 'Blank Cheque' to Austria
document 11

This is the report of the famous conversation between Wilhelm II and the Austrian ambassador in Berlin, Count Szögyény, in which the kaiser seemed to promise his support for Austria under any conditions.

Szögyény to Count Leopold Berchtold (Austro-Hungarian Foreign Minister)

Berlin 5 July 1914   tel.237 Strictly Confidential
... the Kaiser authorised me to inform our gracious majesty that we might in this case, as in all others, rely upon Germany's full support ... he did not doubt in the least that Herr von Bethmann Hollweg would agree with him. Especially as far as our action against Serbia was concerned. But it was his (Kaiser Wilhelm's) opinion that this action must not be delayed. Russia's attitude will no doubt be hostile, but for this he had for years prepared, and should a war between Austria-Hungary and Russia be unavoidable, we might be convinced that Germany, our old faithful ally, would stand at our side. Russia at the present time was in no way prepared for war, and would think twice before it appealed to arms ... if we had really recognised the necessity of warlike action against Serbia, he (Kaiser Wilhelm) would regret if we did not make use of the present moment, which is all in our favour ...

Quoted in Geiss, (**7**), p. 77

Germany's Balkan policy
document 12

Jagow (German secretary of state) to Prince Lichnowsky (German ambassador in London), 18 July 1914. Lichnowsky had been critical of Germany's policy of supporting Austria-Hungary in the Sarajevo crisis.

Austria no longer intends to tolerate the sapping activities of the Serbians, and just as little does she intend to tolerate longer the continuously provocative attitude of her small neighbour at Belgrade ... She fully realizes that she has neglected many opportunities, and that she is still able to act, though in a few years she may no longer be able to do so. Austria is now going to force a showdown with Serbia, and has told us so. During the whole Balkan crisis we mediated successfully in the interest of peace, without forcing Austria to passivity at any of the critical moments. The fact that notwithstanding that we have often, with injustice, been accused of trimming and shuffling, makes no difference to me. Nor have we at the present time forced Austria to her decision. But we neither could nor should attempt to stay her hand. If we should do that, Austria would have the right to reproach us (and we ourselves) with having deprived her of her last chance of political rehabilitation. And then the process of her wasting away and of her internal decay would be still further accelerated. Her standing in the Balkans would be gone forever. You will undoubtedly agree with me that the absolute establishment of the Russian hegemony in the Balkans is, indirectly, not permissible, even for us. The maintenance of Austria, and, in fact, of the most powerful Austria possible, is a necessity for us both for internal and external reasons. That she cannot be maintained forever, I will willingly admit. But in the meantime we may perhaps be able to arrange other combinations.

We must attempt to localise the conflict between Austria and Serbia. Whether we shall succeed in this will depend first on Russia, and secondly on the moderating influence of Russia's allies. The more determined Austria shows herself, the more energetically we support her, so much the more quiet will Russia remain. To be sure, there will be some agitation in St Petersburg, but, on the whole, Russia is not ready to strike at present. Nor will France or England be anxious for war at the present time. According to all competent observation, Russia will be prepared to fight in a few years. Then she will crush us by the number of her soldiers; then she will have built her Baltic Sea fleet and her strategic railroads. Our group, in the meantime, will have become weaker right along.

Quoted in Geiss, (**7**), pp. 122–3

document 13

Russia and the Threat of Revolution

Although some Russians feared that war would result in revolution, most of those in government, as this report by Nicolas de Basily (of the Ministry of Foreign Affairs) on a conversation with Hohenloe (the Austrian military attaché in St Petersburg) shows, felt confident or preferred the risk over humiliation.

One evening in July 1914 ... [Hohenloe and I] took the road out of St. Petersburg toward Finland. The huge forests of black pine were immersed in absolute silence, undisturbed by the slightest breath of air. It was the time of the marvelous white nights of the northern summer. The sun had scarcely disappeared beneath the horizon only to rise again about an hour later. A faint, pale light illuminated the landscape, sad and austere, and increased in us a certain state of anxiety inspired by the recent political news ...

[We] could not turn our thoughts from the tension growing day by day between our two countries. We could already foresee some of the possible consequences of the Sarajevo murder. Taking me by the arm, Hohenloe said, 'Do you understand that you cannot go to war? If you do, you will expose yourself to revolution and to the ruin of your power.' I replied to my friend that while some changes within Russia and perhaps even a serious internal crisis were probable in the future, at present there was no indication of internal trouble. Public opinion was clamoring for an intervention in support of Serbia, and the Russian government would have the approval of the entire nation if it judged itself obliged to act. I added forcefully, 'You commit a serious error of calculation in supposing that fear of a revolution will prevent Russia from fulfilling its national duty now. As for the future, who can predict that with certainty?'

N. de Basily, (**13**), pp. 89–90

document 14

The Policy of Sir Edward Grey

In the 1920s Sir Edward Grey tried to defend himself against charges that he had contributed to the outbreak of war by following a weak and vacillating policy.

Certain things stand out very clearly in my memory of the week before the war. The general suffering and the private griefs of the war have left scars in the memory of all who experienced them; but the week before the war also left marks on those who had responsibility – marks indelible, too deep to be obscured even by the distress of what followed.

What was said or done by me will be most clearly explained and best understood by stating the considerations and convictions that were dominant in my mind throughout that week . . .

1. A conviction that a great European war under modern conditions would be a catastrophe for which previous wars afforded no precedent . . . I thought this must be obvious to everyone else, as it seemed obvious to me; and that, if once it became apparent that we were on the edge, all the Great Powers would call a halt and recoil from the abyss.

2. That Germany was so immensely strong and Austria so dependent upon German strength that the word and will of Germany would at the critical moment be decisive with Austria. It was therefore to Germany that we must address ourselves.

3. That, if war came, the interest of Britain required that we should not stand aside, while France fought alone in the West, but must support her. I knew it to be very doubtful whether the Cabinet, Parliament and the country would take this view on the outbreak of war, and through the whole of this week I had in view the probable contingency that we should not decide at the critical moment to support France. In that event I should have to resign . . .

4. A clear view that no pledge must be given, no hope even held out to France and Russia, which it was doubtful whether this country would fulfil. One danger I saw so hideous that it must be avoided and guarded against at every word. It was that France and Russia might face the ordeal of war with Germany relying upon our support; that this support might not be forthcoming, and that we might then, when it was too late, be held responsible by them for having let them in for a disastrous war . . .

The notion of being involved in war about a Balkan quarrel was repugnant . . . there was no sentiment urging us to go into a war on Serbia's behalf. If France were involved, it would not be in any quarrel in which we owed her good-will . . . It would indeed not be in any quarrel of her own at all; it would be because she, as Russia's Ally, had the misfortune to be involved in a Russian quarrel . . . What, it was asked, was the good of keeping so carefully clear of alliances and obligations if we were to be drawn into European war in such a quarrel as this? ... Some of us felt that the considerations stated above did not touch the true issue. We felt that to stand aside would mean the domination of Germany; the subordination of France and Russia; the isolation of Britain, the hatred of her by both those who had feared and those who had wished for her intervention in the war; and ultimately that Germany would wield the whole power of the Continent. How would she use it as regards Britain? Could anyone feel comfortable about that question? Could anyone give to it truthfully in his heart any but a sinister and foreboding answer?

Viscount Grey, (**31**, Vol. 1), pp. 311–3, 335, 337

document 15

The Austrian ultimatum

The preamble to the ultimatum asserted that the Serbian government was culpable in the assassination because it had tolerated the rise of a subversive movement within its territory and done nothing to prevent its criminal activities.

... the Royal Government finds itself obliged to demand from the Serbian Government an official assurance that it condemns the propaganda directed against Austria-Hungary and in their entirety the dealings whose ultimate aim it is to disjoin parts of the territory belonging to the Monarchy and that it pledges itself to suppress with all the means in its power this criminal and terrorist propaganda.

With a view to giving these assurances a solemn character, the Royal Serbian Government will publish the following declaration on the first page of its official press-organ of 26/13 July:

'The Royal Serbian Government condemns the propaganda directed against Austria-Hungary, that is the entirety of the ambitions, whose ultimate aim it is to disjoin parts of the territory belonging to the Austrian-Hungarian Monarchy and regrets sincerely the horrible consequences of these criminal ambitions.

The Royal Serbian Government regrets that Serbian officers and officials have taken part in the propaganda above-mentioned and thereby imperilled the friendly and neighbourly relations, which the Royal Government had solemnly promised to cultivate in its declaration of 31 March 1909.

The Royal Government, which condemns and rejects every thought and every attempt to interfere in behalf of the inhabitants of any part of Austria-Hungary, considers it a duty to warn officers, officials and indeed all the inhabitants of the kingdom, that it will in future use great severity against such persons, as will be found guilty of similar doings, which the Government will make every effort to suppress.'

This declaration will at the same time be communicated to the Royal army by an order of His Majesty the King, and will besides be published in the official organ of the army.

The Royal Serbian Government will overmore pledge itself to the following:

1. To suppress every publication likely to inspire hatred and contempt against the Monarchy or whose general tendencies are directed against the integrity of the latter;

2. to begin immediately dissolving the society called *Narodna odbrana*; to seize all its means of propaganda and to act in the same way against all the societies and associations in Serbia, which are busy with the propaganda against Austria-Hungary; the Royal Government will take the necessary measures to prevent these societies continuing their efforts under another name or in another form;

3. to eliminate without delay from public instruction everything that serves or might serve the propaganda against Austria-Hungary, both where teachers or books are concerned;

4. to remove from military service and from the administration all officers and officials who are guilty of having taken part in the propaganda against Austria-Hungary, whose names and the proofs of whose guilt the Imp. and Royal Government will communicate to the Royal Government;

5. to consent that Imp. and Royal Officials assist in Serbia in the suppressing of the subversive movement directed against the territorial integrity of the Monarchy;

6. to have a judicial enquiry instituted against all those who took part in the plot of 28 June, if they are to be found on Serbian territory; the Imp. and Royal Government will delegate organs who will take an active part in these enquiries;

7. to arrest without delay Major Voija Tankosić and a certain Milan Ciganović, a Serbian government official, both compromised by the results of the enquiry;

8. to take effective measures so as to prevent the Serbian authorities from taking part in the smuggling of weapons and explosives across the frontier; to dimiss from service and severely punish those organs of the frontier service at Schabatz and Loznica, who helped the perpetrators of the crime of Sarajevo to reach Bosnia in safety;

9. to give the Imp. and Royal Government an explanation of the unjustified remarks of high Serbian functionaries in Serbia as well as in foreign countries, who, notwithstanding their official positions, did not hesitate to speak in hostile terms of Austria-Hungary in interviews given just after the event of 28 June;

10. to inform the Imp. and Royal Government without delay that the measures summed up in the above points have been carried out.

Quoted in Geiss, (**7**), pp. 144–5

document 16

The Russian mobilisation

The French Ambassador in St. Petersburg, Maurice Paléologue, recorded Russia's explanation of her decision to commence a general mobilisation.

29 July

At eleven o'clock tonight, Nicholas-Alexandrovitch Basily, Deputy-Director of the chancellery of the Foreign Office, appeared at my embassy. He came to tell me that the imperious language used by the German Ambassador this afternoon has decided the Russian Government (1) to order this very night the mobilization of the thirteen corps earmarked for operations against Austria-Hungary; (2) secretly to commence general mobilization.

These last words made me jump:

'Isn't it possible for them to confine themselves – provisionally at any rate – to a partial mobilization?'

'No. The question has just been gone into thoroughly by a council of our highest military officers. They have come to the conclusion that in existing circumstances the Russian Government has no choice between partial and general mobilization as from the technical point of view a partial mobilization could be carried out only at the price of dislocating the entire machinery of general mobilization. So if to-day we stopped at mobilizing the thirteen corps destined for operations against Austria and tomorrow Germany decided to give her ally military support, we should be powerless to defend ourselves on the frontiers of Poland and East Prussia.'

M. Paléologue, (**43**), p. 32

Chronology of events

1871	10 May, Treaty of Frankfurt: end of Franco-Prussian war
1879	7 October, Dual Alliance signed by Germany and Austria-Hungary
1881	18 June, *Dreikaiserbund* signed
1882	20 May, Italy joins Germany and Austria-Hungary in Triple Alliance
1887	18 June, Russo-German Reinsurance Treaty signed
1887	12 December, First Mediterranean agreement: Great Britain, Austria-Hungary and Italy
1888	15 June, Wilhelm II becomes emperor
1890	15 March, Bismarck dismissed
1890	18 June, Reinsurance treaty not renewed
1891	27 August, Russo-French political agreement
1894	4 January, Russo-French military alliance ratified
1897	27 April, Russia and Austria-Hungary agree to put Balkans 'on ice'
1902	30 January, Anglo-Japanese alliance signed
1903	2 October, Russia and Austria-Hungary conclude the Murzsteg agreement
1904	8 February, Japan attacks Russia
1904	8 April, Anglo-French entente
1905	27 May, Battle of Tsushima
1905	24 July, Treaty of Björkö
1905	5 September, Treaty of Portsmouth ends Russo-Japanese war
1906	16 January, Algeçiras Conference begins
1906	7 April, Algeçiras Act signed
1907	31 August, Anglo-Russian entente
1908	16 September, Buchlau agreement between Izvolsky and Aehrenthal
1908	6 October, Bosnia and Herzegovina annexed by Austria-Hungary
1909	8 February, Franco-German agreement on Morocco
1911	1 July, German gunboat *Panther* arrives in Agadir

1911   4 November, Franco-German agreement on Morocco
1912   13 March, Alliance signed between Serbia and Bulgaria
1912   29 May, Greece joins Serbia and Bulgaria in 'Balkan
            League'
1912   18 October, First Balkan War begins
1913   30 May, Treaty of London ends First Balkan War
1913   29 June, Second Balkan War begins
1913   11 August, Treaty of Bucharest ends Second Balkan War
1914   28 June, Archduke Franz Ferdinand assassinated at
            Sarajevo
1914   28 July, Austria declares war on Serbia
1914   28 July, Russia orders 'partial' mobilisation
1914   30 July, Russia orders general mobilisation for following
            day
1914   30 July, Austria orders general mobilisation for following
            day
1914   31 July, German ultimatum to Russia
1914   1 August, Germany declares war on Russia
1914   3 August, Germany declares war on France
1914   4 August, Britain declares war on Germany

Bibliography

COLLECTIONS OF DOCUMENTS

1 *auswärtige Politik Serbiens, Die: 1903–14*, ed. M. Bogitschew-itsch, 3 vols, Berlin, 1928–31.
2 *British Documents on the Origins of the War*, G. P. Gooch and H. Temperley (eds), 11 vols, London, 1927–38.
3 *documenti diplomatici italiani, I: 1861–1914*, 4th and 5th series, ed. A. Torre, Rome, 1954, 1964.
4 *Documents Diplomatiques Françaises: 1871–1914*, 2ᵉ Serie (Paris, 1930–35), 3ᵉ Serie, Paris, 1929–36.
5 *German Diplomatic Documents: 1871–1914*, ed. and trans. E. T. S. Dugdale, 4 vols, London and New York, 1928.
6 *Grosse Politik der Europäischen Kabinette: 1871–1914*, J. Lepsius, ed. A. Mendellsohn-Bartholdy and F. Thimme, 39 vols, Berlin, 1922.
7 *July 1914. Selected Documents*, ed. I. Geiss, Batsford, 1967.
8 *Österreich-Ungarns Aussenpolitik von der Bosnischen Krise 1908 bis zum Kriegsausbruch 1914*, ed. L. Bittner, A. Pribram, H. Srbik and H. Uebersberger, 8 vols. Vienna, 1930.

AUTOBIOGRAPHIES, MEMOIRS AND DIARIES

9 Agathon, *Les jeunes gens d'aujourd'hui*, Paris, 1913.
10 Abrikossow, D.I., *Revelations of a Russian Diplomat*, Seattle, 1964.
11 Asquith, H. H., *Genesis of the War*, London, 1923.
12 Barthélemy, J., *Démocratie et politique étrangère*, Paris, 1917.
13 Basily, N. de, *Diplomat of Imperial Russia*, Hoover Institute Press, 1973.
14 Bismarck, Otto von, *Die gesammelten Werke* (ed. H. von Petersdorff *et. al.*), 15 vols, Berlin, 1923–33.
15 Bogitshevich, M., *The Causes of the War*, London, 1920.
16 Bülow, B. von, *Memoirs*, 4 vols, trans. F. A. Voigt, Putnam, 1930–32.
17 Caillaux, J., *Mes mémoires*, 3 vols, Paris, 1942–47.
18 Cambon, J., *The Diplomat*, London, 1931.

19 Cambon, P., *Correspondance 1870–1914*, ed. H. Cambon, 3 vols, Paris, 1940–46.

20 Chirol, V., *Fifty Years in a Changing World*, London, 1927.

21 Churchill, W. S., *The World Crisis 1911–18*, 2 vols, New American Library, 1968.

22 Ebel, G. (ed.), *Botschafter Paul Graf von Hatzfeldt Nachgelassene Papiere 1838–1901*, 2 vols, Boppard, 1976.

23 Eckardstein, H. von, *Lebenserinnerungen und Politische Denkwürdigkeiten*, 3 vols, Leipzig, 1919–21.

24 Erdmann, K. D. (ed.), *Kurt Riezler: Tagebücher, Aufsätze, Dokumente*, Göttingen, 1972.

25 Fellner, F. (ed.) *Das politische Tagebüch Josef Redlichs*, Vienna, 1953.

26 George, D. Lloyd, *The War Memoirs of David Lloyd George*, 6 vols, London, 1933–36.

27 Gérard, A., *Mémoires d'Auguste Gérard*, Paris, 1928.

28 Giers, N. K., *The Education of a Russian Statesman*, ed C. and B. Jelavich, California, 1962.

29 Giolitti, G., *Memoirs of my Life*, London, 1923.

30 Grant, N. F., *The Kaiser's Letters to the Tsar*, Hodder and Stoughton, 1920.

31 Grey, E., *Twenty-five Years 1892–1916*, 2 vols, Hodder and Stoughton, 1925.

32 Haldane, R. B., *Before the War*, London, 1920.

33 Hoetzendorf, Conrad von F., *Aus meiner Dienstzeit*, 4 vols, Vienna, 1921.

34 Hardinge of Penshurst, Lord, *Old Diplomacy*, London, 1947.

35 Isvolsky, A. P., *The Memoirs of Alexander Iswolski*, Academic International, 1974.

36 Kalmykov, A. D., *Memoirs of a Russian Diplomat*, Yale, 1971.

37 Kokovtsov, V. N., *Out of My Past*, Stanford, 1935.

38 Lichnowsky, Prince, *My Mission to London*, London, 1918.

39 Loreburn, Lord, *How the War Came*, London, 1919.

40 Messimy, A., *Mes souvenirs*, Paris, 1937.

41 Morley, J., *Memorandum on Resignation, August 1914*, London, 1928.

42 Neklyudov, A. V., *Diplomatic Reminiscences*, London, 1920.

43 Paléologue, M., *An Ambassador's Memoirs*, 3 vols, Hutchinson, 1923–25.

44 Paléologue, M., *The Turning Point: three critical years, 1904–06*, London, 1935.

45 Poincaré, R., *The Origins of the War*, London, 1922.

46 Poincaré, R., *Memoirs*, 4 vols, London, 1926–30.

47 Przibram, L. Ritter von, *Erinnerungen eines alten Oesterreichers*, 2 vols, Stuttgart, 1912.

48 Redlich, J. (ed.), *J. M. Baernreither: Fragmente eines politischen Tagebüchs*, Berlin, 1928.

49 Rich, N. and Fisher, M. H. (eds), *The Holstein Papers*, 4 vols, Cambridge University Press, 1955–63.

50 Ringhoffer, K. (ed.), *The Bernstorff Papers*, 2 vols, London, 1908.

51 Rosen, Baron R. R., *Forty Years of Diplomacy*, 2 vols, London, 1922.

52 Saint Aulare, Comte de, *Confession d'un vieux diplomate*, Paris, 1953.

53 Salandra, A., *Italy and the Great War, from Neutrality to Intervention*, London, 1932.

54 Sazonov, S., *Fateful Years 1909–16*, Jonathan Cape, 1928.

55 Schebeko, N., *Souvenirs*, Paris, 1936.

56 Schmoller, G. von, *Zwanzig Jahre deutscher Politik 1897–1917*, Munich and Leipzig, 1920.

57 Sonnino, S., *Diario* (eds B. F. Brown and P. Pastorelli), 3 vols, Bari, 1972.

58 Tirpitz, A. von, *My Memoirs*, 2 vols, London, 1919.

59 Tittoni, T., *Italy's Foreign and Colonial Policy*, London, 1915.

60 Varé, D, *Laughing Diplomat*, London, 1938.

GENERAL BOOKS

61 Albertini, Luigi, *The Origins of the War of 1914*, 3 vols, London, 1964.

62 Allain, J.-C., *Agadir 1911, une crise impérialiste en Europe pour la conquête du Maroc*, Paris, 1976.

63 Anderson, E. N., *The First Moroccan Crisis, 1904–06*, Chicago, 1930.

64 Anderson, M. S., *The Eastern Question*, Macmillan, 1966.

65 Barlow, I. C., *The Agadir Crisis*, Durham, N. C., 1940.

66 Bayer, T. A., *England und der neue Kurs, 1890–95*, Tübingen, 1955.

67 Bridge, F. R., *Great Britain and Austria-Hungary, 1906–14*, Weidenfeld and Nicolson, 1972.

68 Bridge, F. R. and Bullen, R., *The Great Powers and the European States System, 1815–1914*, Longman, 1980.

69 Carlgren, W. M., *Iswolsky und Aehrenthal vor der bosnischen Annexionskrise*, Uppsala, 1955.

70 Churchill, R. P., *The Anglo-Russian Convention of 1907*, Cedar Rapids, Iowa, 1939.

71 Crampton, R. J., *The Hollow Détente: Anglo-German Relations in the Balkans, 1911–14*, G. Prior, 1980.

72 Decleva, E., *Da Adua a Sarajevo. La Politica estera italiana e la Francia 1896–1914*, Bari, 1971.

73 Dedijer, V., *The Road to Sarajevo*, London, 1967.

74 Droz, J., *Les causes de la première guerre mondiale: essai d'historiographie*, Paris, 1973.

75 Earle, E. M., *Turkey, the Great Powers and the Baghdad Railway*, New York, 1923.

76 Fay, S. B., *The Origins of the World War*, 2 vols, New York, 1928.

77 Gillard, David, *The Struggle for Asia 1828–1914: a study in British and Russian imperialism*, Methuen, 1977.

78 Hale, O. J., *Publicity and Diplomacy: with special reference to England and Germany, 1890–1914*, New York, 1940.

79 Halpern, P., *The Mediterranean Naval Situation, 1908–14*, Cambridge, Mass., 1971.

80 Helmreich, E. C., *The Diplomacy of the Balkan Wars*, Cambridge, Mass., 1938.

81 Hinsley, F. H., *Power and the Pursuit of Peace*, Cambridge University Press, 1963.

82 Howard, H. N., *The Partition of Turkey: a diplomatic history, 1913–23*, New York, 1966.

83 Joll, J., *The Unspoken Assumptions*. London, 1968.

84 Kennedy, P. (ed.), *The War Plans of the Great Powers 1880–1914*, Allen and Unwin, 1979.

85 Koch, H. W. (ed.), *The Origins of the First World War: great power rivalry and war aims*, Macmillan, 1972.

86 Langer, W. L., *European Alliances and Alignments, 1871–90*, New York, 1950.

87 Langhorne, R. T. B., *The Collapse of the Concert of Europe: international politics, 1890–1914*, London, 1981.

88 Mosse, W. E., *The European Powers and the German Question, 1848–1871*, Cambridge University Press, 1958.

89 Nish, I., *The Anglo-Japanese Alliance: the diplomacy of two island empires, 1894–1907*, Greenwood Press, 1977.

90 Petrovich, M. B., *A History of Modern Serbia*, 2 vols, New York, 1976.

91 Poidevin, R., *Les origines de la première guerre mondiale*, Paris, 1975.

92 Poidevin, R. and Bariéty, J., *Les relations franco-allemandes, 1815–1975*, Paris, 1977.

93 Remak, J. (ed.), *The Origins of World War I, 1870–1914*, New York, 1967.

94 Röhl, J. C. G., *1914: delusion or design*, Elek, 1973.

95 Rolo, P. J. V., *Entente Cordiale: the origins and negotiation of the Anglo–French agreements of 8 April 1904*, Macmillan, 1969.

96 Salvatorelli, L., *La triplice alleanza, storia diplomatica*, Milan, 1939.

97 Schmitt, B. E., *The Coming of the War, 1914*, 2 vols, New York, 1930.

98 Taylor, A. J. P., *The Struggle for Mastery in Europe, 1848–1914*, Oxford University Press, 1954.

99 Taylor, A. J. P., *War by Time-table: how the First World War began*, Macdonald, 1969.

100 Turner, L. C. F., *Origins of the First World War*, Edward Arnold, 1970.

101 White, J. A., *The Diplomacy of the Russo- Japanese War*, Princeton, 1965.

102 Williamson, S., *The Politics of Grand Strategy: Britain and France prepare for war, 1904–14*, Cambridge, Mass., 1969.

GENERAL ARTICLES

103 Andrew, C. M., 'German world policy and the reshaping of the Dual Alliance', *Journal of Contemporary History*, I (1966).

104 Andrew, C. M., 'The Entente Cordiale from its origins to 1914', in N. Waites (ed.), *Troubled Neighbours: Franco-British relations in the twentieth century*, London, 1971.

105 Askew, W. C., 'The Austro-Italian antagonism, 1896–1914', in L. P. Wallace and W. C. Askew (eds), *Power, Public Opinion and Diplomacy.* Durham, N. C., 1959.

106 Bergonzi, B., 'Before 1914: writers and the threat of war', *Critical Quarterly*, 6 (1964).

107 Bovykin, V. I., 'The Franco-Russian alliance', *History*, lxiv (1979).

108 Corrigan, H. S. W., 'German–Turkish relations and the outbreak of war in 1914: a reassessment', *Past and Present*, 36 (1967).

109 Dakin, Douglas, 'The diplomacy of the great powers and the Balkan states, 1908–1914', *Balkan Studies*, iii, no. 2 (1962), pp. 327–74.

110   Edwards, E. W., 'The Japanese alliance and the Anglo-French Agreement of 1904', *History*, xlii (1957).

111   Edwards, E. W., 'The Franco-German Agreement on Morocco, 1909', *English Historical Review*, lxxviii (1963).

112   Farrar, L. L., 'Importance of omnipotence: the paralysis of the European great power system, 1871–1914', *International Review of History and Political Science*, ix (1972).

113   Gordon, Michael R., 'Domestic conflict and the origins of the First World War: the British and the German cases', *Journal of Modern History*, xlvi (June 1974), pp. 191–226.

114   Greaves, R. L., 'Some Aspects of the Anglo-Russian convention and its working in Persia, 1907–14', *Bulletin of the School of Oriental and African Studies*, xxxi (1968).

115   Guillen, P. G., 'Les questions coloniales dans les relations franco-allemandes à la veille de la première guerre mondiale', *La Revue Historique* (1972).

116   Hargreaves, J. D., 'The Origins of the Anglo-French military conversations in 1905', *History*, xxxvi (1951).

117   Hatton, P. H. S., 'The First World War: Britain and Germany in 1914, the July crisis and war aims', *Past and Present*, 36 (1967).

118   Hatton, P. H. S., 'Harcourt and Solf: the search for an Anglo-German understanding through Africa 1912–14', *European Studies Review*, i (1971).

119   Hering, Gunnar, 'Die serbisch bulgarische Beziehungen am Vorabend der Balkan kreige', *Balkan Studies*, iii (1962), pp. 297–326.

120   Hillgruber, A., 'Die "Krieg-in-sicht" – krise 1875', in E. Schulin (ed.), *Gedenkschrift Martin Göhring, Studien zur europäischen Geschichte*. Wiesbaden, 1968.

121   Hinsley, F. H., 'Bismarck, Salisbury and the Mediterranean agreements of 1887', *The Historical Journal*, i (1958), pp. 76–80.

122   Joll, J., 'War guilt 1914: a continuing controversy', in P. Kluke and P. Alter (eds), *Aspekte der deutsch–britischen Beziehungen in Laufe der Jahrhunderte*. Stuttgart, 1978.

123   Joll, J., 'Politicians and the freedom to choose: the case of July 1914', in A. Ryan (ed.), *The Idea of Freedom, essays in honour of Isaiah Berlin*. Oxford, 1979.

124   Koch, H. W., 'The Anglo-German alliance negotiations, missed opportunity or myth', *History*, liv (Oct. 1969), pp. 378–92.

125 Long, J., 'Franco-Russian Relations during the Russo-Japanese war', *Slavonic and East European Review*, lii (1974).

126 Mayer, Arno, 'Domestic origins of the First World War', in L. Krieger and F. Stern (eds), *The Responsibility of Power*. New York, 1967.

127 Mayer, S. L., 'Anglo-German rivalry at the Algeciras Conference', in P. Gifford and W. R. Louis (eds), *Britain and Germany in Africa*. New Haven, Conn., 1967.

128 Oppel, B. F., 'The waning of a traditional alliance: Russia and Germany after the Portsmouth peace conference', *Central European History*, 5 (1972).

129 Prevelakis, Elentherios, 'Elentherios Venizelos and the Balkan wars', *Balkan Studies*, vii (1966), pp. 363–78.

130 Remak, Joachim, '1914 – the Third Balkan War, origins reconsidered', *Journal of Modern History*, xliii (Sept 1971), pp. 353–66.

131 Schroeder, Paul W., 'World War I as "Galloping Gertie": a reply to Joachim Remak', *Journal of Modern History*, xliv (Sept 1972), pp. 319–45.

132 Steinberg, J., 'Diplomatie als Wille und Vorstellung: Die Berliner Mission Lord Haldanes in Februar 1912', in H. Schottelius and W. Deist (eds), *Marine und Marinepolitik im kaiserlichen Deutschland 1871–1914*, Düsseldorf, 1972.

133 Stone, N., 'Moltke–Conrad: Relations between the Austro-Hungarian and German general staffs, 1909–14', *Historical Journal*, x (1966).

134 Sweet, D. W., 'The Bosnian crisis', in F. H. Hinsley (ed.), *British Foreign Policy under Sir Edward Grey*. Cambridge, 1977.

135 Towle, P., 'The European balance of power in 1914', *Army Quarterly and Defence Journal*, 104 (1974).

136 Turner, L. C. F., 'The role of the general staffs in July 1914', *Australian Journal of Politics and History* (1965).

137 Valiani, L., 'Italian–Austro-Hungarian negotiations, 1914–15', *Journal of Contemporary History*, i (1966).

138 Williams, Beryl J., 'The strategic background to the Anglo-Russian entente of August 1907', *The Historical Journal*, ix (1966), pp. 360–73.

139 Wilson, Keith, 'The Agadir crisis, the Mansion House speech and the double-edgedness of agreements', *The Historical Journal*, xv (1972), pp. 513–32.

140 Xantalos, Diogenis, 'The Greeks and the Turks on the eve of the Balkan wars', *Balkan Studies*, iii (1962), pp. 277–96.

GERMANY

Books

141 Berghahn, V. R., *Der Tirpitz Plan: Genesis und Verfall einer innenpolitischen Krisenstrategie unter Wilhelm II*, Dusseldorf, 1971.
142 Berghahn, V. R., *Germany and the Approach of War in 1914*, Macmillan, 1973.
143 Berghahn, V. R., *Militarismus*, Cologne, 1975.
144 Calleo, D., *The German Problem Reconsidered*, Cambridge University Press, 1978.
145 Carroll, E. M., *Germany and the Great Powers, 1866–1914: a study in public opinion and foreign policy*, New York, 1938.
146 Craig, G. A., *Germany, 1866–1945*, Oxford University Press, 1978.
147 Dehio, Ludwig, *Germany and World Politics in the Twentieth Century*, New York, 1959.
148 Deist, W., *Flottenpolitik und Flottenpropaganda*, Stuttgart, 1976.
149 Eyck, E., *Bismarck and the German Empire*, Allen and Unwin, 1968.
150 Fischer, Fritz, *Germany's Aims in the First World War*, Chatto, 1967.
151 Fischer, Fritz, *War of Illusions*, Chatto, 1975.
152 Geiss, I., *German Foreign Policy, 1871–1914*, Routledge, 1976.
153 Guillen, P., *L'Allemagne et le Maroc de 1870 à 1905*, Paris, 1967.
154 Hauser, O., *Deutschland und der englisch–russische Gegensatz, 1900–14*, Göttingen, 1958.
155 Hillgruber, A., *Bismarcks Aussenpolitik*, Freiburg, 1972.
156 Jarausch, K. H., *The Enigmatic Chancellor*, Yale, 1973.
157 Kitchen, M., *The German Officer Corps, 1890–1914*, Oxford University Press, 1968.
158 Messerschmidt, M., *Militär und Politik in der Bismarckzeit und im Wilhelminischen Deutschland*, Darmstadt, 1975.
159 Moritz, A., *Das Problem des Präventivkrieges in der deutschen Politik während der ersten Marokkokrise*, Frankfurt A. M., 1974.
160 Nicholls, J. A., *Germany after Bismarck: the Caprivi era, 1890–94*, New York, 1968 edn.
161 Rich, N., *Friedrich von Holstein: politics and diplomacy in the era of Bismarck and Wilhelm II*, 2 vols, Cambridge University Press, 1965.
162 Ritter, G., *The Schlieffen Plan*, Wolff, 1958.
163 Schottelius, H. and Deist, W., *Marine und Marinepolitik im Kaiserlichen Deutschland, 1871–1914*, Düsseldorf, 1972.

164 Smith, Woodruff D., *The German Colonial Empire*, Chapel Hill, 1978.

165 Steinberg, J., *Yesterday's Deterrent: Tirpitz and the birth of the German battle fleet*, Macdonald, 1965.

166 Trumpener, Ulrich, *Germany and the Ottoman Empire, 1914–18*, Princeton, 1968.

167 Vogel, B., *Deutsche Russlandpolitik 1900–06*, Düsseldorf, 1973.

168 Winzen, P., *Bülow's Weltmachtkonzept*, Boppard A. R., 1977.

Articles

169 Barkin, K. D., 'Conflict and concord in Wilhelmian social thought', *Central European History*, 5 (1972).

170 Chickering, Roger, 'Patriotic societies and German foreign policy, 1890–1914', *International History Review*, i (1979), pp. 470–489.

171 Crampton, R. J., 'The Balkans as a factor in German foreign policy, 1911–1914', *The Slavonic and East European Review*, lv (1977), pp. 370–90.

172 Eley, G., 'Sammlungspolitik, social imperialism and the Navy Law of 1898', *Militärgeschichtliche Mitteilungen*, i (1974).

173 Ganz, A. Harding, 'The German navy in the Far East and Pacific: the seizure of Kiatschow and after', in J. Moses and P. M. Kennedy (eds), *Germany in the Pacific and Far East 1870–1914*. St. Lucia, Queensland, 1977.

174 Jarausch, K., 'The illusion of limited war: Chancellor Bethmann Hollweg's calculated risk, July 1914', *Central European History*, 2 (1969).

175 Kennedy, P. M., 'Tirpitz, England and the second Navy Law of 1900: a strategical critique', *Militärgeschichtliche Mitteilungen*, 2 (1970).

176 Kennedy, Paul M., 'German world policy and the alliance negotiations with England, 1897–1900', *Journal of Modern History*, xlv (1973), pp. 605–25.

177 Kennedy, Paul M., 'The development of German naval operations plans against England, 1896–1914', *English Historical Review*, lxxxix (1974), pp. 48–76.

178 Mortimer, Joanna Stafford, 'Commercial interests and German diplomacy in the Agadir crisis', *The Historical Journal*, x (1967), pp. 440–56.

179 Steinberg, Jonathan, 'The Copenhagen complex', *Journal of Contemporary History*, i (1966), pp. 23–46.

180 Steinberg, J., 'The novella of 1908: necessities and choices in the Anglo-German naval arms race', *Transactions of the Royal Historical Society*, 5th ser., xxi (1971).

181   Stern, F., 'Bethmann Hollweg and the war: the limits of responsibility', in L. Krieger and F. Stern (eds), *The Responsibility of Power*. Garden City, NY, 1967.

182   Trumpener, U., 'Liman von Sanders and the German Ottoman alliance', *Journal of Contemporary History*, i (1966).

183   Turner, L. C. F., 'The significance of the Schlieffen plan', *Australian Journal of Politics and History*, xiii (1967).

AUSTRIA- HUNGARY

Books

184   Bridge, F. R., *From Sadowa to Sarajevo*, Routledge, 1972.

185   Hantsch, H., *Leopold, Graf Berchtold*, 2 vols, Graz, 1963.

186   Lafore, L., *The Long Fuse*, Weidenfeld and Nicolson, 1966.

187   Macartney, C. A. *The Habsburg Monarchy, 1790–1918*, Weidenfeld and Nicolson, 1968.

188   May, A. J., *The Hapsburg Monarchy, 1867–1914*, Harvard, 1965.

189   Pribram, A., *Austrian Foreign Policy, 1908–18*, London, 1923.

Articles

190   Bradley, J. F. N., 'Czech Pan-Slavism before the First World War', *Slavonic and East European Review*, xl (1961).

191   Bridge, F. R., '*Tarde venientibus ossa*: Austro-Hungarian colonial aspirations in Asia Minor, 1913–14', *Middle Eastern Studies*, (1970).

192   Bridge, F. R., 'Izvolsky, Aehrenthal and the end of the Austro-Russian entente, 1906–08', *Mitteilungen des oesterreichischen Staatsarchivs*, xxix (1976), pp. 315–62.

193   Bridge, F. R., 'Austria-Hungary and the Balkan states, 1906–1908', in F. H. Hinsley (ed), *British Foreign Policy under Sir Edward Grey*. Cambridge, 1977.

194   Fellner, F., 'Die Haltung Oesterreich–Ungarns während der Konferenz von Algeciras, 1906', *Mitteilungen des Instituts für österreichische Geschichtsforschung*, 71 (1963).

195   Peterson, M. B. A., 'Das österreichischen-ungarische Memorandum an Deutschland vom 5 July 1914', *Scandia*, 30 (1964).

196   Stone, N., 'Hungary and the crisis of July 1914', *Journal of Contemporary History*, i (1966).

197 Turczynski, E., 'Oesterreich-Ungarn und Südosteuropa während der Balkan kriege', *Balkan Studies*, v (1964), pp. 11–46.

198 Wank, Solomon, 'Aehrenthal and the Sanjak railway project: a reappraisal', *The Slavonic and East European Review*, xlii (1964), pp. 354–96.

ITALY

Books

199 Askew, W. C., *Europe and Italy's Acquisition of Libya, 1911–12*, Durham, N.C., 1959.

200 Bosworth, R. J. B., *Italy, the least of the Great Powers: Italian foreign policy before the First World War*, New York, 1979.

201 Bosworth, R. J., *Italy and the Approach of the First World War*, Macmillan, 1983.

202 Coppa, F. J., *Planning, Protectionism and Politics in Liberal Italy: economics and politics in the Giolittian age*, Washington, 1971.

203 Drake, R., *Byzantium for Rome: the politics of nostalgia in Umbertian Italy, 1878–1900*, Chapel Hill, 1980.

204 Glanville, J. L., *Italy's Relations with England, 1896–1905*, Baltimore, 1934.

205 Hess, R. L., *Italian Colonialism in Somalia*, Chicago, 1966.

206 Lowe, C. J. and Marzari, F., *Italian Foreign Policy, 1870–1940*, Routledge, 1975.

207 Mack Smith, D., *Italy, A modern history*, rev. ed. Ann Arbor, 1969.

208 Salomone, A. W., *Italy in the Giolittian Era: Italian democracy in the making, 1900–14*, Philadelphia, 1960.

209 Thayer, J. A., *Italy and the Great War, politics and culture, 1870–1915*, Madison, 1964.

210 Webster, R. A., *Industrial Imperialism in Italy, 1908–1915*, Berkeley, 1975.

Articles

211 Cunsolo, R. S., 'Libya, Italian nationalism and the revolt against Giolitti', *Journal of Modern History*, 37 (1963).

212 Hess, R. L., 'Italy and Africa: colonial ambitions in the First World War', *Journal of African History*, iv (1963).

213 Renzi, W. A., 'Italy's neutrality and entrance into the Great War: a re-examination', *American Historical Review*, lxxiii (1967–8).

107

214 Tamborra, A., 'The rise of Italian industry and the Balkans (1900–14)', *Journal of European Economic History*, 3 (1974).

RUSSIA

Books

215 Lieven, D. C. B., *Russia and the Origins of the First World War*, Macmillan, 1983.

216 Seton-Watson, R. W., *The Russian Empire, 1801–1917*, Oxford University Press, 1967.

217 Thaden, E. C., *Conservative nationalism in nineteenth-century Russia*, Seattle, 1964.

218 Thaden, E. C., *Russia and the Balkan alliance of 1912*, Pennsylvania, 1965.

219 Walicki, A., *The Slavophile Controversy*, Oxford University Press, 1975.

220 Westwood, J. N., *Endurance and Endeavour: Russian history, 1812–1980*, Oxford University Press, 1981.

Articles

221 Bestuzhev, I. V., 'Russian foreign policy, February–June 1914', *Journal of Contemporary History*, i (1966).

222 Hutchinson, J. F., 'The Octobrists and the future of Russia as a great power', *Slavonic and East European Review*, 1 (1972).

223 Turner, L. C. F., 'The Russian mobilization of 1914', *Journal of Contemporary History*, ii (1968), pp. 65–88.

FRANCE

Books

224 Anderson, R. D., *France, 1870–1914, politics and society*, Routledge, 1977.

225 Andrew, Christopher, *Théophile Delcassé and the Making of the Entente Cordiale, 1898–1905*, Macmillan, 1968.

226 Auffray, B., *Pierre de Margerie et la vie diplomatique de son temps*, Paris, 1976.

227 Becker, J.-J., *1914, comment les Français sont entrés dans la guerre*, Paris, 1977.

228 Bouvier, J. and Girault, R. (eds), *L'impérialisme français d'avant 1914*, Paris, 1976.

229 Brogan, D. W., *The Development of Modern France, 1870–1939*, Hamish Hamilton, 1940.

230 Brunschwig, H., *French Colonialism, 1871–1914: myths and realities*, London, 1966.

231 Bury, J. P. T., *France, 1814–1940*, 4th edn., Methuen, 1969.

232 Carroll, E. M., *French Public Opinion and Foreign Affairs, 1870–1914*, London, 1931.

233 Contamine, H., *La Revanche, 1871–1914*, Paris, 1957.

234 Duroselle, J.-B., *La France et les Français, 1900–1914*, Paris, 1972.

235 Eubank, Keith, *Paul Cambon, master diplomatist*, Norman, Okla, 1960.

236 Ganiage, J., *L'Expansion coloniale de la France sons la Troisième République 1871–1914*, Paris, 1968.

237 Girardet, R., *Le nationalisme français, 1871–1914*, Paris, 1966.

238 Girardet, R., *L'idée coloniale en France de 1871 à 1962*, Paris, 1972.

239 Girault, R., *Emprunts russes et investissements français en Russie, 1887–1914*, Paris, 1973.

240 Mitchell, Alan, *The German Influence in France after 1870: the formation of the French Republic*, Chapel Hill, 1979.

241 Poidevin, R., *Finances et relations internationales, 1887–1914*, Paris, 1970.

242 Porch, D., *The March to the Marne*, Cambridge University Press, 1981.

243 Thobie, J., *Intérêts et impérialisme français dans l'empire Ottoman, 1895–1914*, Paris, 1977.

244 Weber, E., *The Nationalist revival in France, 1905–1914*, Berkeley, Calif., 1959.

Articles

245 Allain, J.-C., 'L'expansion française au Maroc de 1902 à 1912', in J. Bouvier and R. Girault (eds), *L'imperialisme français d'avant 1914*. Paris, 1976.

246 Andrew, C. M., 'The French colonialist movement during the Third Republic: the unofficial mind of imperialism', *Transactions of the Royal Historical Society*, 5th ser., xxvi (1976).

247 Andrew, C. M. and Kanya-Forstner, A. S., 'The French "Colonial Party": its composition, aims and influence, 1885–1914', *The Historical Journal*, xiv (1971).

248 Andrew, C. M., 'Gabriel Hanotaux, the Colonial Party and the Fashoda strategy', *Journal of Imperial and Commonwealth History*, iii (1974).

249 Cairns, J. C., 'International politics and the military mind:

the case of the French Republic, 1911–14', *Journal of Modern History* (1953).

250 Girault, R., 'Les Balkans dans les relations franco-russes en 1912', *La Revue Historique* (1975).

BRITAIN

Books

251 Bourne, K., *The Foreign Policy of Victorian England 1830–1902*, Oxford University Press, 1970.

252 Busch, Briton Cooper, *Hardinge of Penshurst: a Study in the old diplomacy*, Hamden, Conn., 1980.

253 Busch, B. C., *Britain and the Persian Gulf, 1894–1914*, Berkeley, 1967.

254 Gooch, J., *The Plans of War: the general staff and British military strategy, 1907–16*, Oxford University Press, 1974.

255 Grenville, J. A. S., *Lord Salisbury and Foreign Policy: the close of the nineteenth century*, Athlone Press, 1964.

256 Howard, C. H. D., *Splendid isolation*, Macmillan, 1967.

257 Lowe, C. J., *Salisbury and the Mediterranean, 1886–96*, Routledge, 1965.

258 Lowe, C. J. and Dockrill, M. C. (eds), *The Mirage of Power*, 3 vols. Routledge, 1972.

259 Marder, A. J., *British Naval Policy, 1880–1905: the anatomy of British sea power*, London, 1940.

260 Monger, G. W., *The End of Isolation: British foreign policy, 1900–1907*, Nelson, 1963.

261 Steiner, Z. S., *The Foreign Office and Foreign Policy, 1898–1914*, Cambridge University Press, 1969.

262 Steiner, Z. S., *Britain and the Origins of the First World War*, Macmillan, 1977.

Articles

263 Best, G. F. A., 'Militarism and the Victorian public schools', in B. Simon and I. Bradley (eds), *The Victorian Public School*. London, 1975.

264 Butterfield, H., 'Sir Edward Grey in July 1914', *Irish Historical Studies*, v (1965).

265 Cooper, M. B., 'British policy in the Balkans, 1908–1909', *The Historical Journal*, vii (1964), pp. 258–79.

266 Cosgrave, Richard, 'A note on Lloyd George's speech at the Mansion House, 21 July 1911', *The Historical Journal*, xii (1966), pp. 698–701.

267   Cosgrove, R. A., 'The Career of Sir Eyre Crowe: a reassessment', *Albion*, iv (1972).

268   Dockrill, M. L., 'British policy during the Agadir crisis of 1911', in F. H. Hinsley (ed.), *The Foreign Policy of Sir Edward Grey*. Cambridge, 1977.

269   Ekstein, M., 'Sir Edward Grey and Imperial Germany in 1914', *Journal of Contemporary History*, vi (1971).

270   French, David, 'The Edwardian crisis and the origins of the First World War', *International History Review*, iv (1982), pp. 207–21.

271   Grenville, J. A. S., 'Lansdowne's abortive project of 12 March 1901 for a secret agreement with Germany', *Bulletin of the Institute of Historical Research*, xxvii (1954).

272   Haggie, P., 'The Royal Navy and war planning in the Fisher era', *Journal of Contemporary History*, viii (1973).

273   Lammers, D., 'Arno Mayer and the British decision for war', *Journal of British Studies*, xii (1973).

274   Mackay, R. F., 'The Admiralty, the German navy, and the redistribution of the British fleet, 1904–1905', *Mariner's Mirror*, 56 (1970), pp. 341–46.

275   Meacham, S., 'The sense of an impending clash: English working-class unrest before the First World War', *American Historical Review*, 77 (1972).

276   Steiner, Z. S., 'The Great Britain and the creation of the Anglo-Japanese alliance', *Journal of Modern History*, xxxi (1959).

277   Steiner, Z. S., 'Grey, Hardinge and the Foreign Office, 1905–10', *The Historical Journal*, x (1967), pp. 415–39.

278   Watt, D. C., 'British press reactions to the assassination at Sarajevo', *European Studies Review*, i (1971).

279   Wilson, K. M., 'The British cabinet's decision for war', *British Journal of International Studies*, i (1975).

280   Wilson, K. M., 'To the Western Front: British war plans and the "military entente" with France before the First World War', *British Journal of International Studies*, iii (1977), pp. 151–68.

281   Wilson, T., 'Britain's "Moral Commitment" to France in August 1914', *History*, lxiv (1979).

Index